Parts of me are STILL AMAZING

Photos & Stories

CATHRYN WELLNER

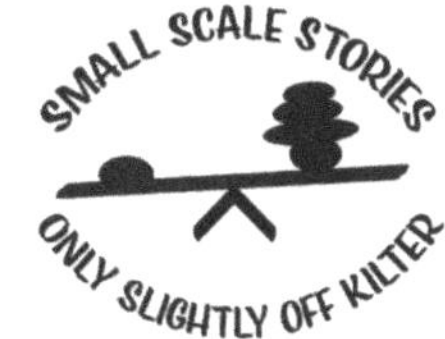

Small Scale Stories #2
Espoir Press
British Columbia 2017

Espoir Press
1002 - 1128 Sunset Drive
Kelowna, British Columbia
Canada V1Y 9W7

Parts of Me Are Still Amazing (Small Scale Stories #2)

ISBN 978-1-988760-03-2

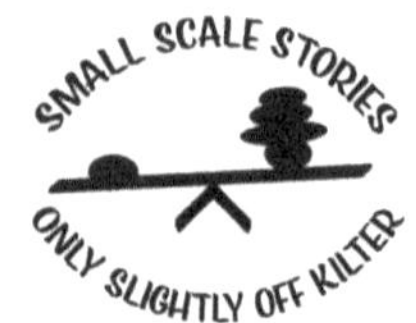

INTRODUCTION

Somewhere between our first fascination with body parts and our final breath, self-consciousness sets in. We learn about body shaming.

Photoshopped models become icons of perfection. We jump on the latest body-shaping, pounds-reducing trends. We groan at our cellulite, oddly shaped fingers, bowed legs, and cowlicks.

Our bodies do not measure up to elusive ideals. We know we are inadequate.

And yet...every single one of us is unique. We are incredibly special.

Reality check: I told myself all this supposedly reassuring trivia on a daily basis. I was not reassured. I was so far from airbrushed perfection no amount of photo editing could set me straight.

So I started paying attention to irregularities and decay around me. My camera caught fading flowers, oddly shaped clouds, and awkward birds.

They reassured me. If I could look admiringly at a rotting pumpkin, a one-legged chicken, and a rheumy-eyed crow, surely I could at least accept the perfectly imperfect figure in the mirror.

Putting together this book made me laugh at my body insecurities. I hope it will do the same for you.

So...welcome to Book #2 in the series: Small Scale Stories - Only Slightly Off Kilter. May you find a laugh, a rueful nod, and maybe even a smidgen of reassurance in its pages.

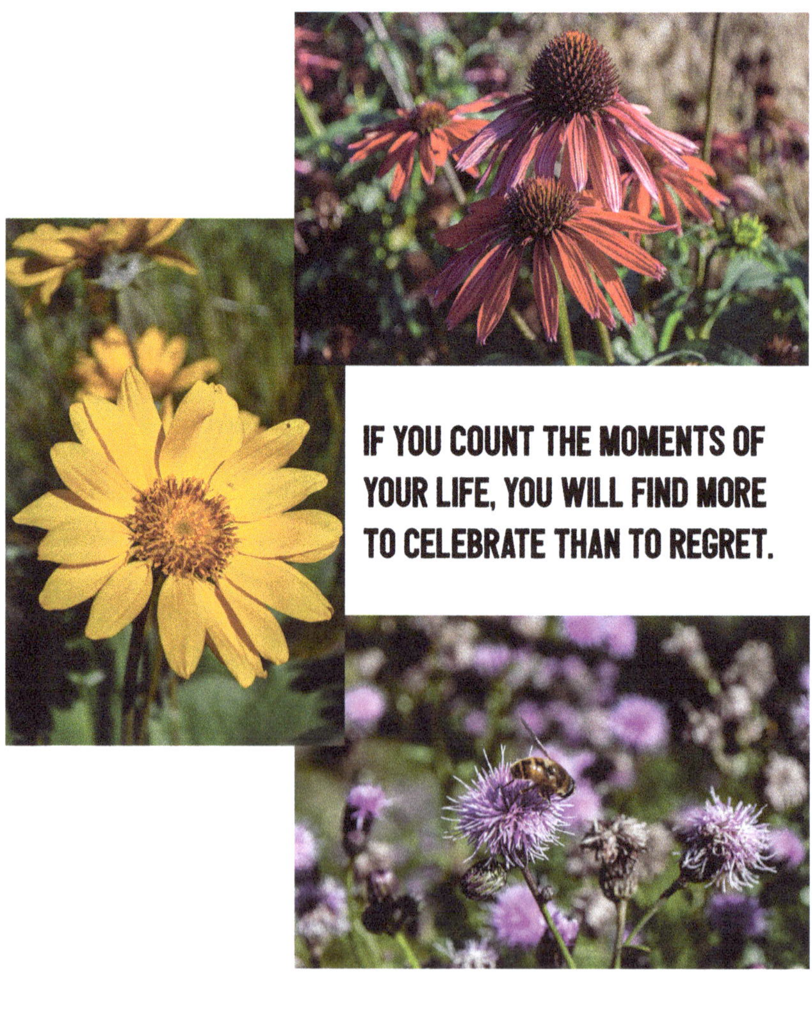
IF YOU COUNT THE MOMENTS OF YOUR LIFE, YOU WILL FIND MORE TO CELEBRATE THAN TO REGRET.

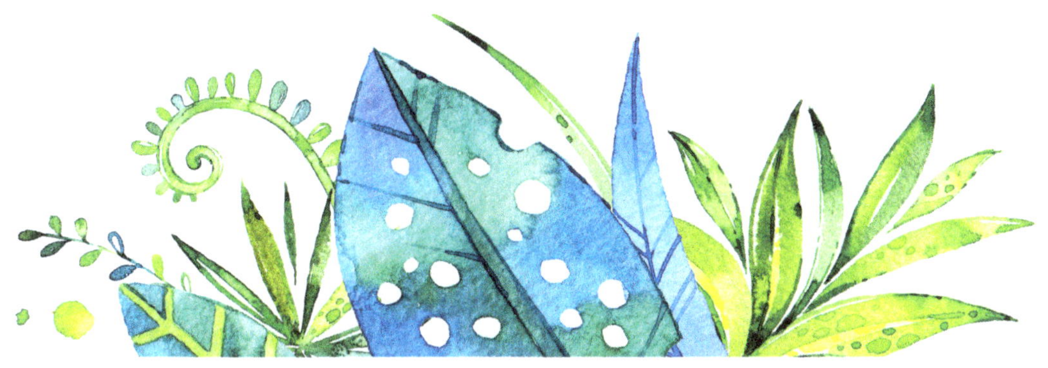

For Robin Jarman, whose youthful heart delights me.
Yours is the only photo of a human in this book. You're
a perfect fit in a collection of small-scale stories
focused on making the best of what life sends our way.

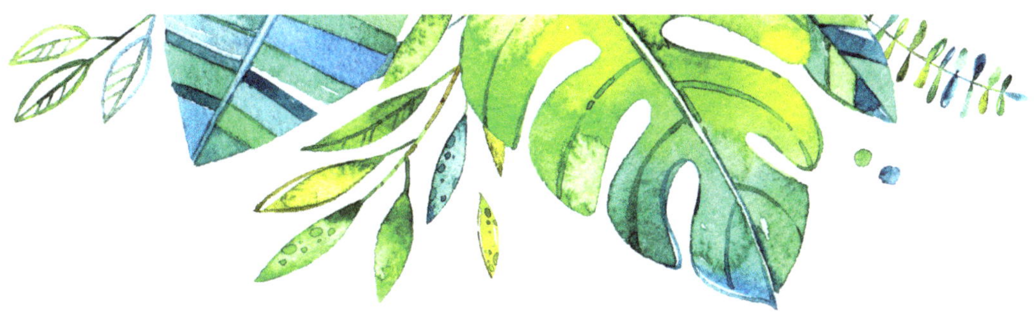

THE STORIES

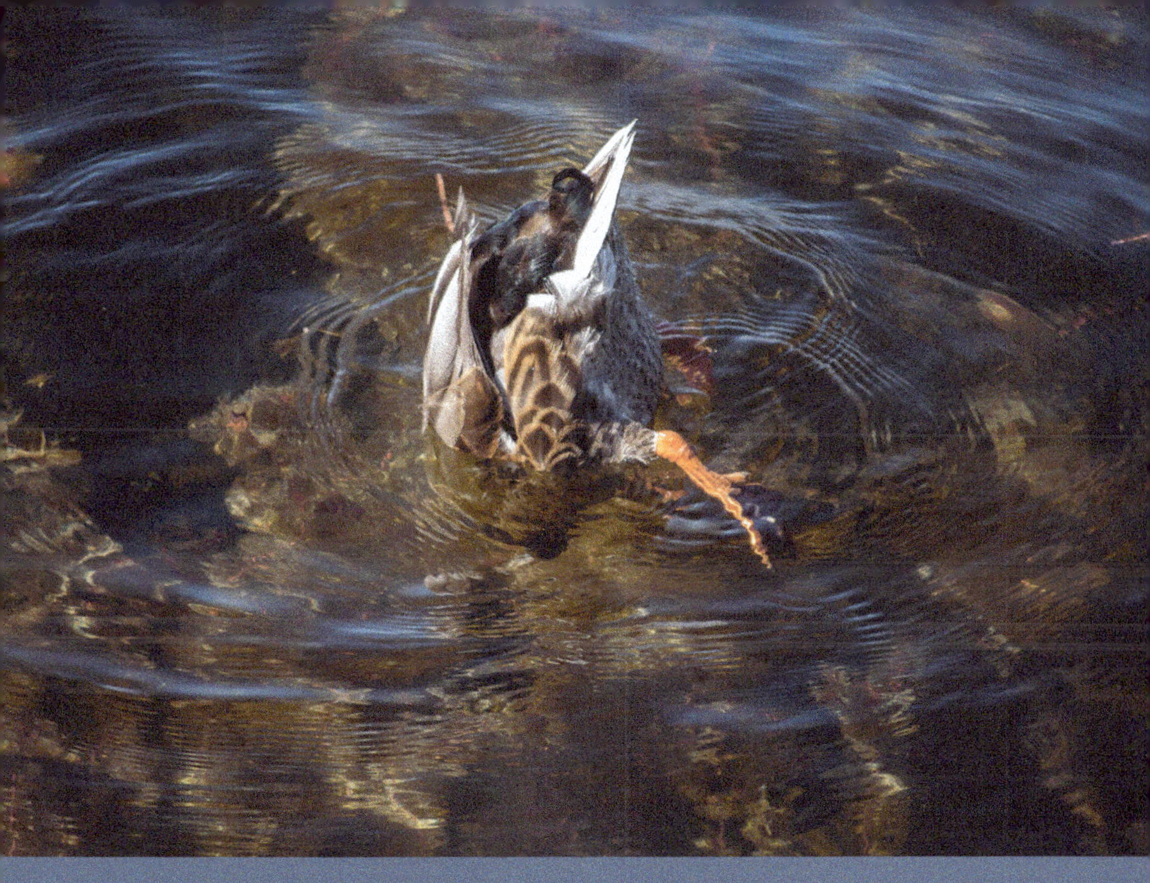

The humans saw only an invasive weed, to be pulled out and destroyed. Mallard saw yummy millefeuille and all the tasty treats hidden in her waving fronds. Perspective is everything.

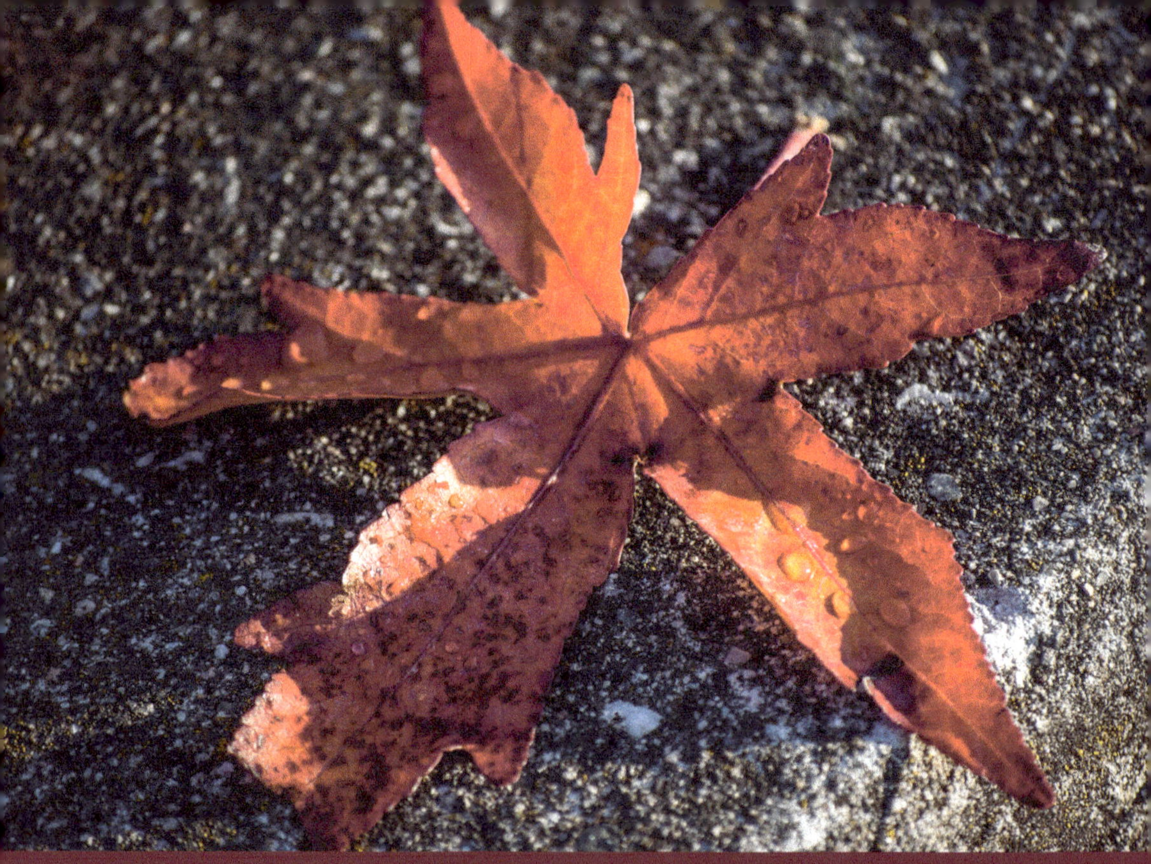

Her life had begun that spring, as a small bud pushing through a tree limb. Now she had retired from months of shade duty. Ready for adventure, she asked Wind to take her where she had never been before.

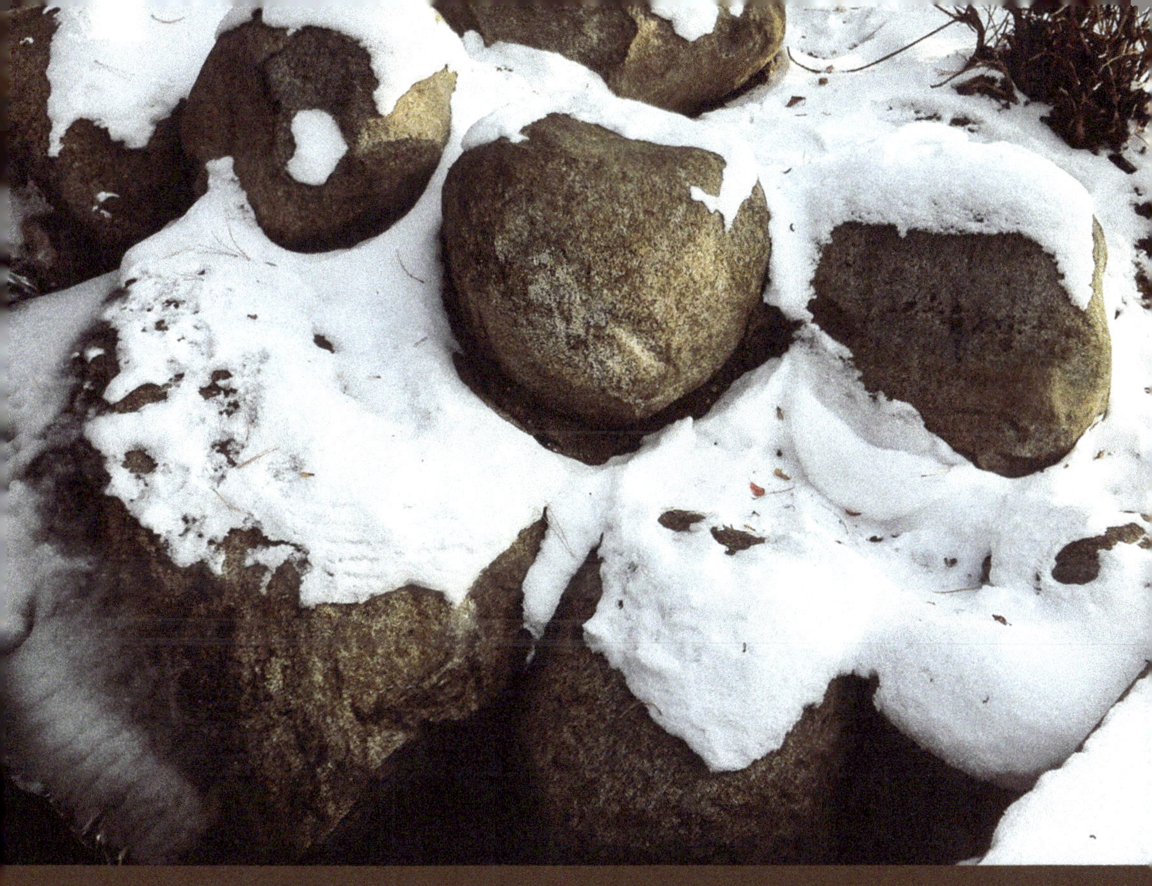

Rocks were having the best time. Snow had drawn a moustache on them and even a pupil on one. Ice was working on a beard. They were becoming Old Man of the Rocks and couldn't stop laughing.

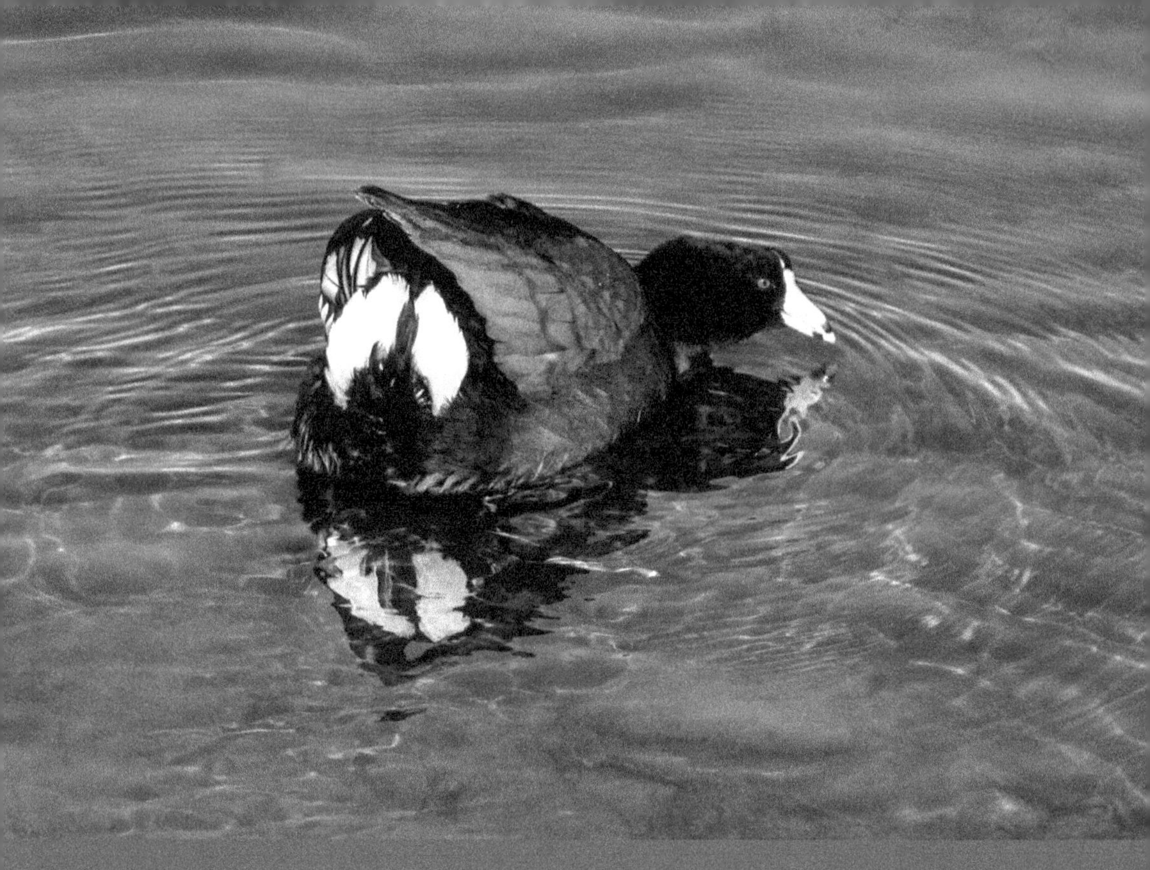

Everyone thought of Coot as rather plain and drab. But when he was excited, he showed his vibrant heart...or, rather, his patterned rump.

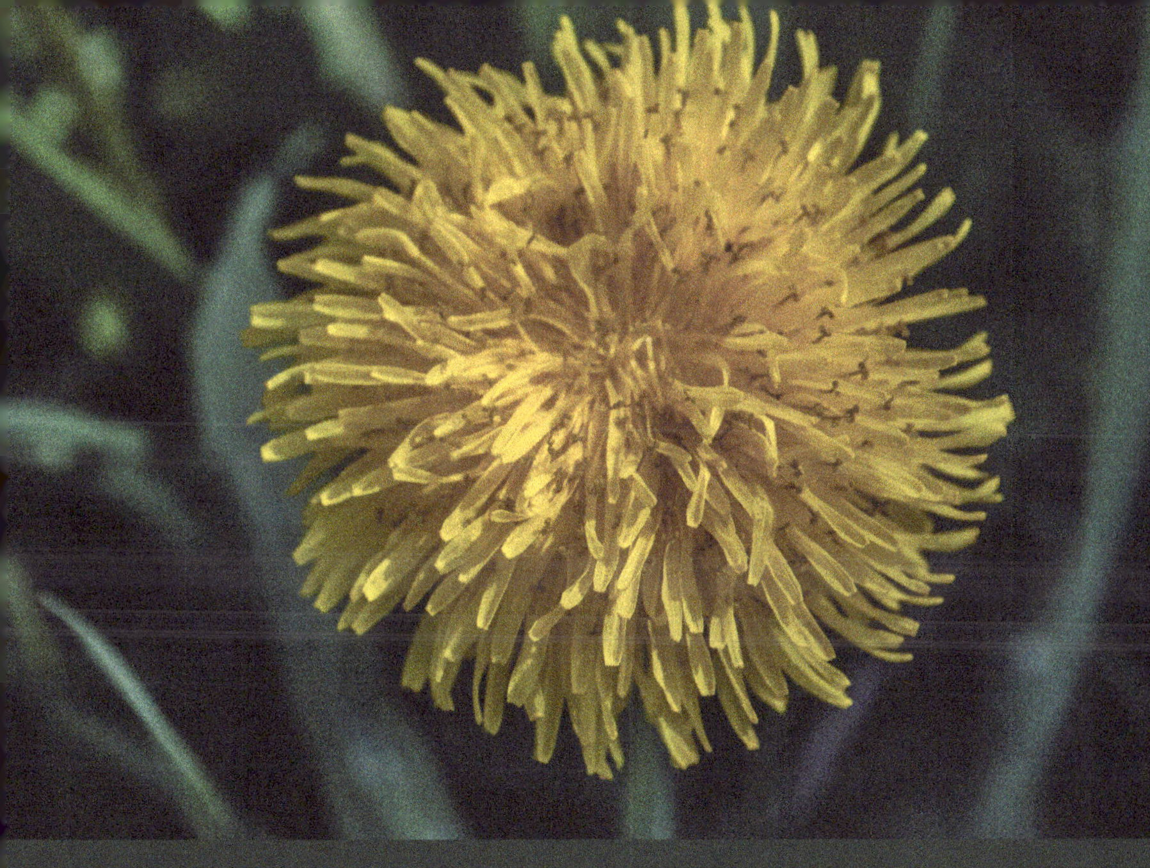

No matter how many times they told her, "You're only a weed," no matter how many times they sprayed her with poison, Dandelion knew she was a gift. She kept on giving, freely, generously, without hope of recompense.

The misshapen parsnip was overlooked repeatedly until a four-year-old insisted on taking him home. They had hours of fun playing Headless Horseman before Parsnip joined carrots and onions in a tasty soup.

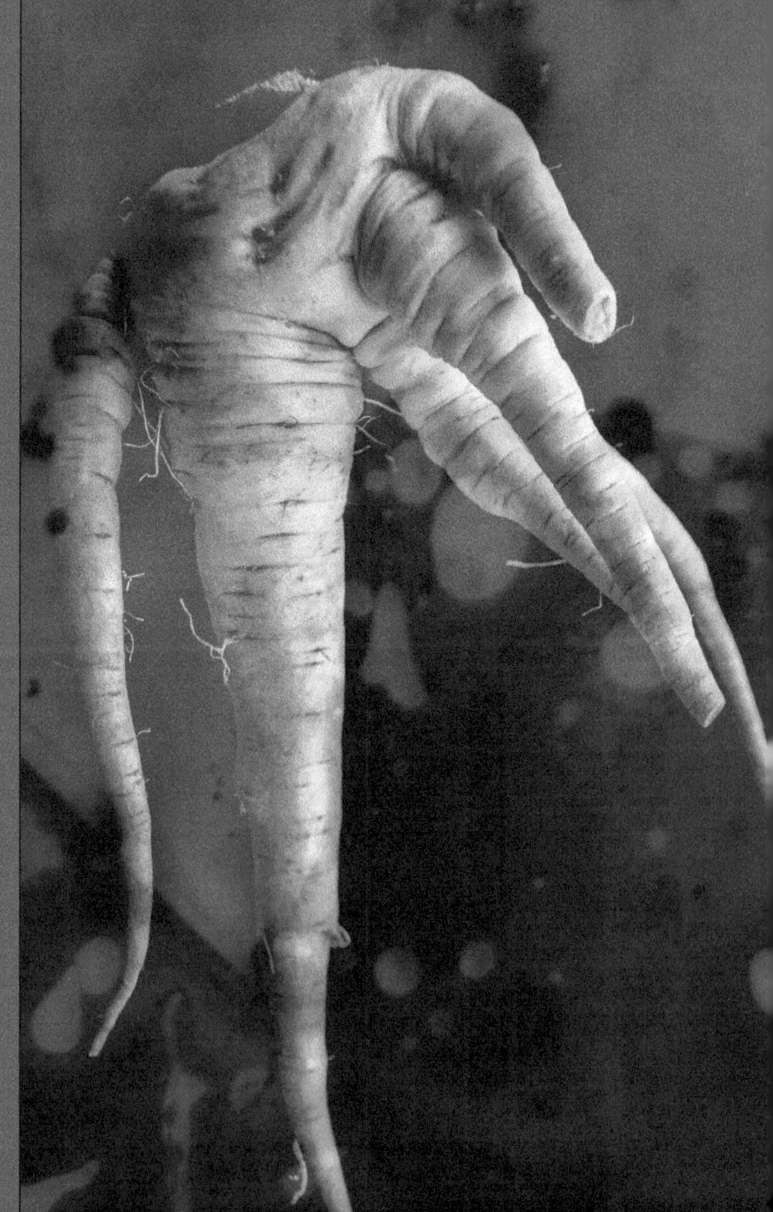

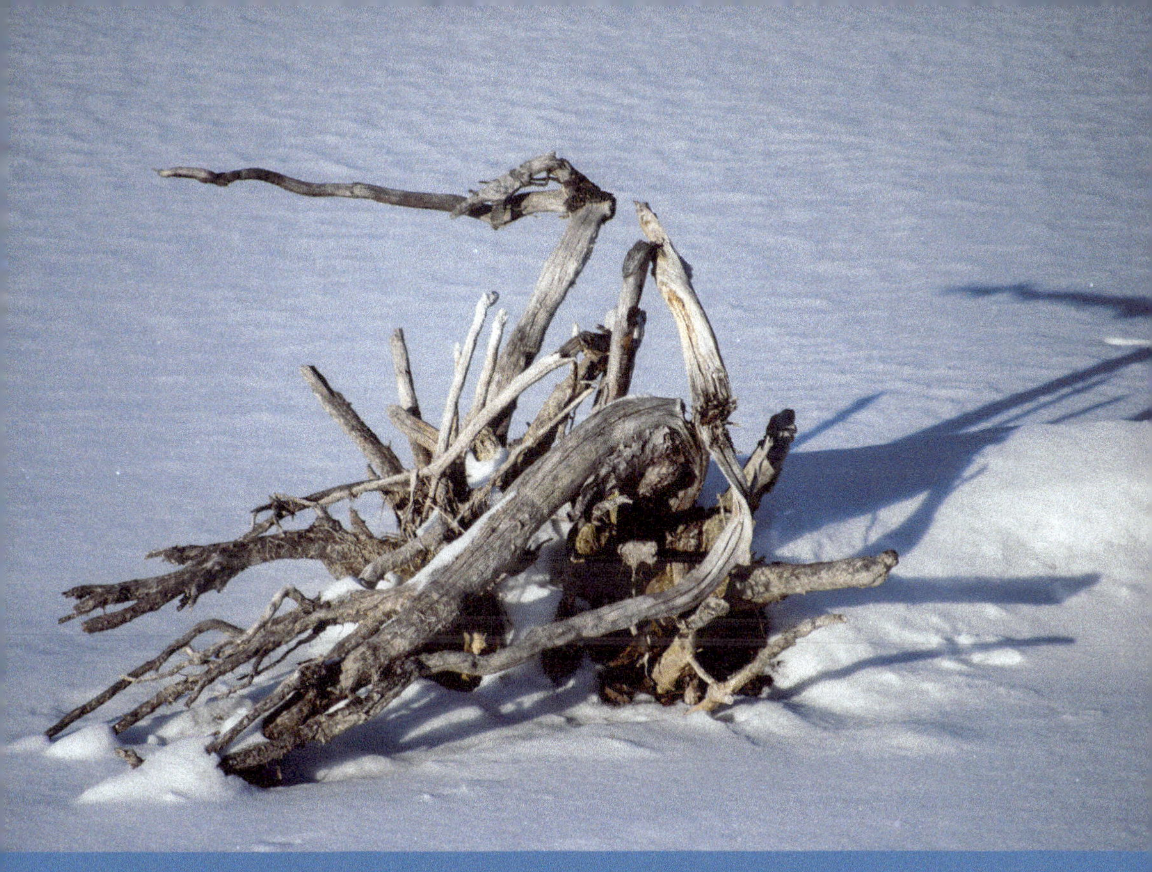

Today she was Veronica, motorcycle-riding wild woman, hair streaming, fans clamoring to be near her. Nothing could stop her now.

Some thought her foliage was dead, but dead and golden are two different things. She had spread her roots beneath the pavers and would soon be changing her winter dress for new greenery.

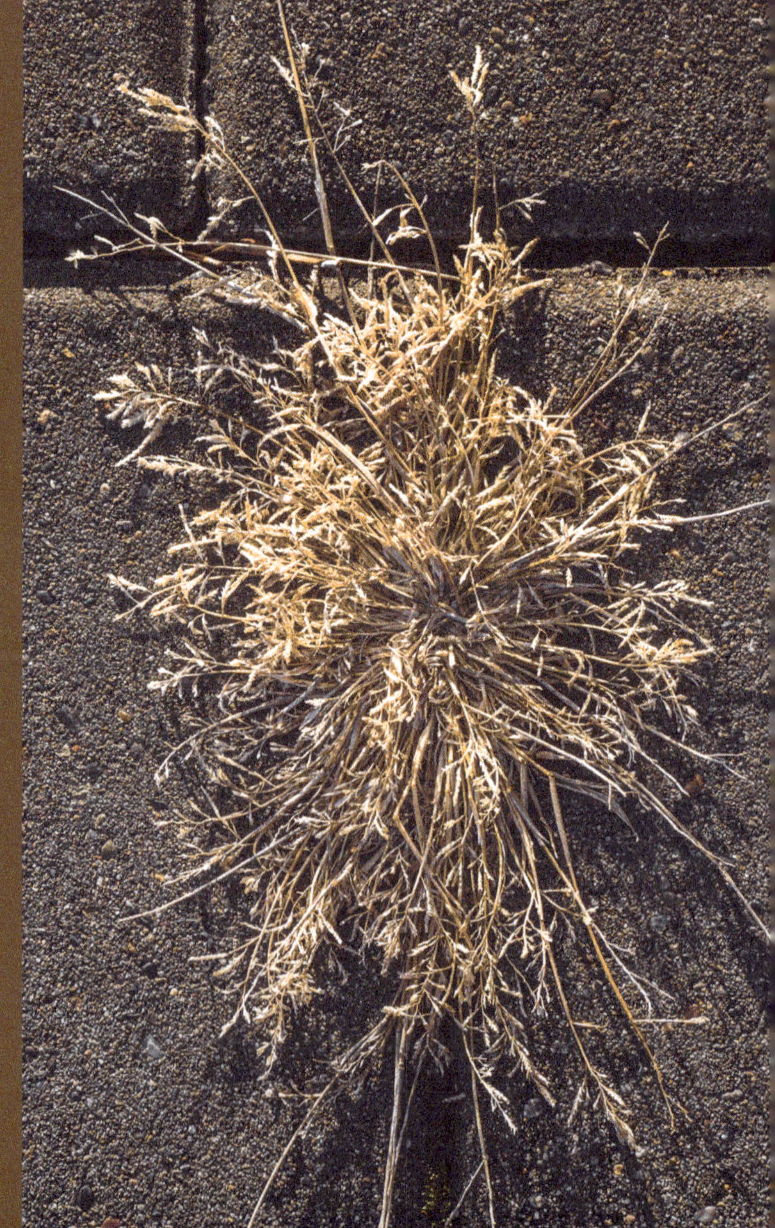

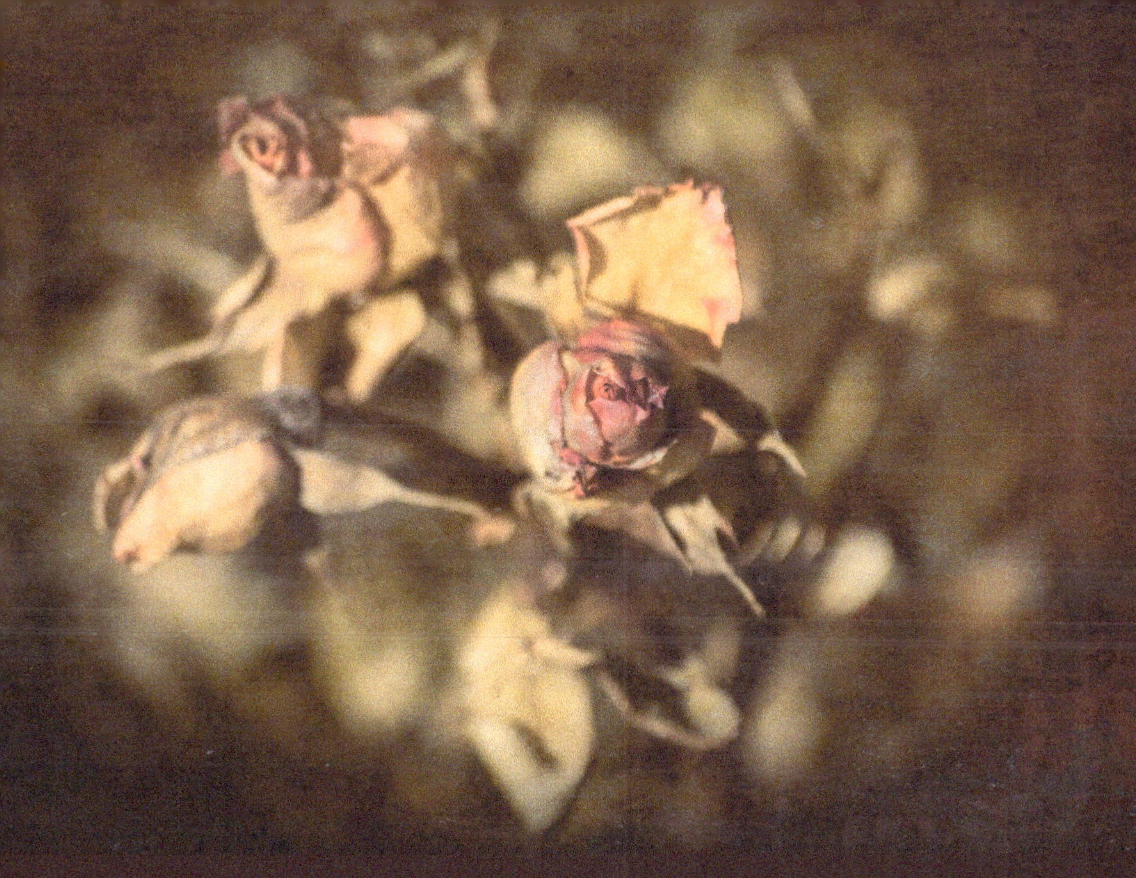

They called her "old, decayed, past her prime."
She laughed at their folly. She was vintage, and
vintage was in fashion.

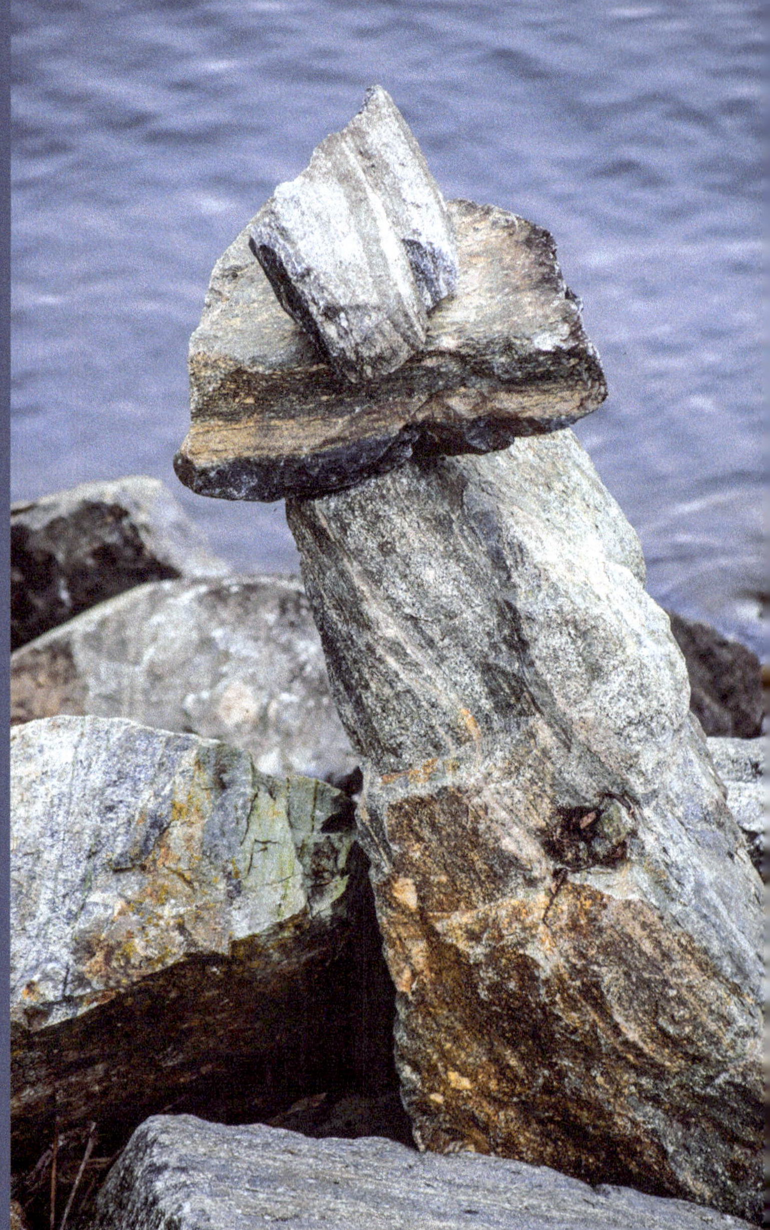

"If one more beer-drinking joker makes a rude comment about my shape," vowed Inukshuk, "I'll topple right onto his foot."

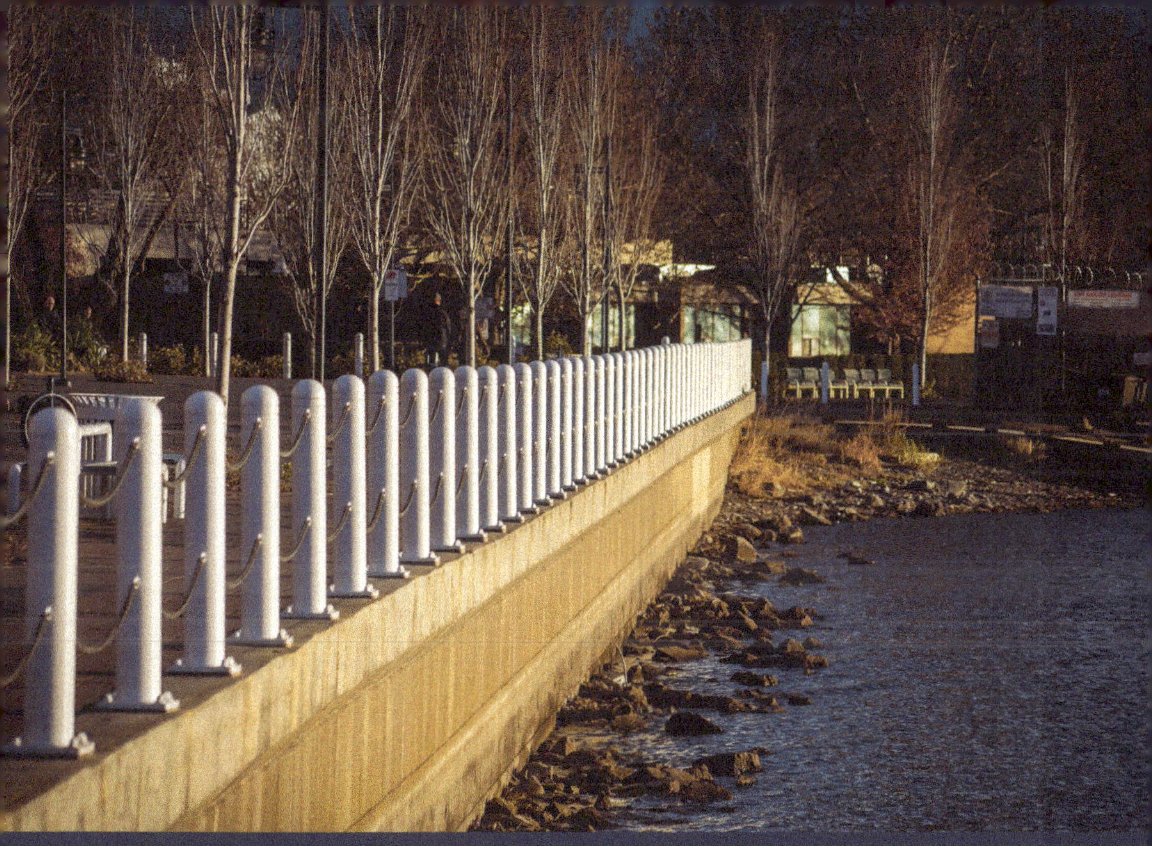

In the beginning, Posts had lined up perfectly. But Ground began tickling Wall. Wall began shivering with silly delight. Perfection gave way to wobbles. Posts laughed and decided to just enjoy it all.

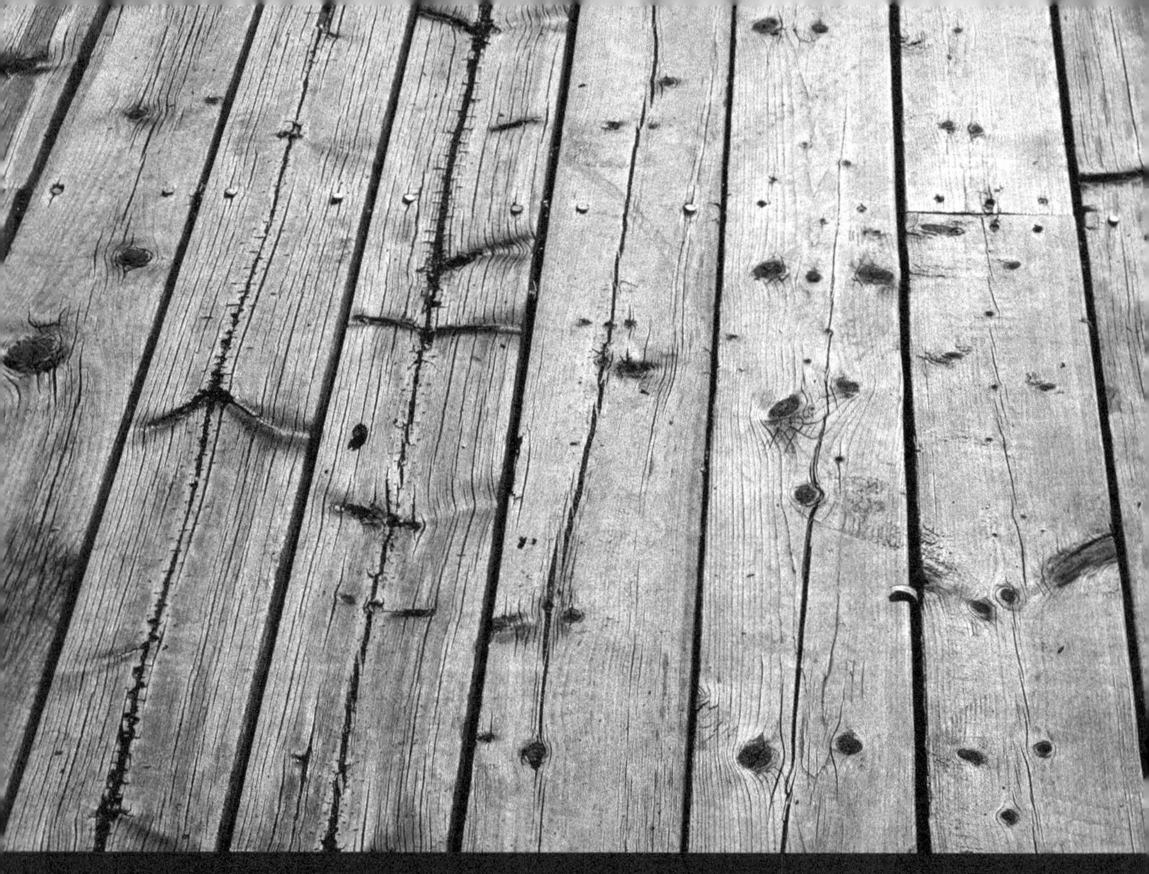

When they were first laid side by side, they grumbled about the people walking on them so heedlessly. Gradually, they began sharing stories of their days in different forests. Now life was exciting once again.

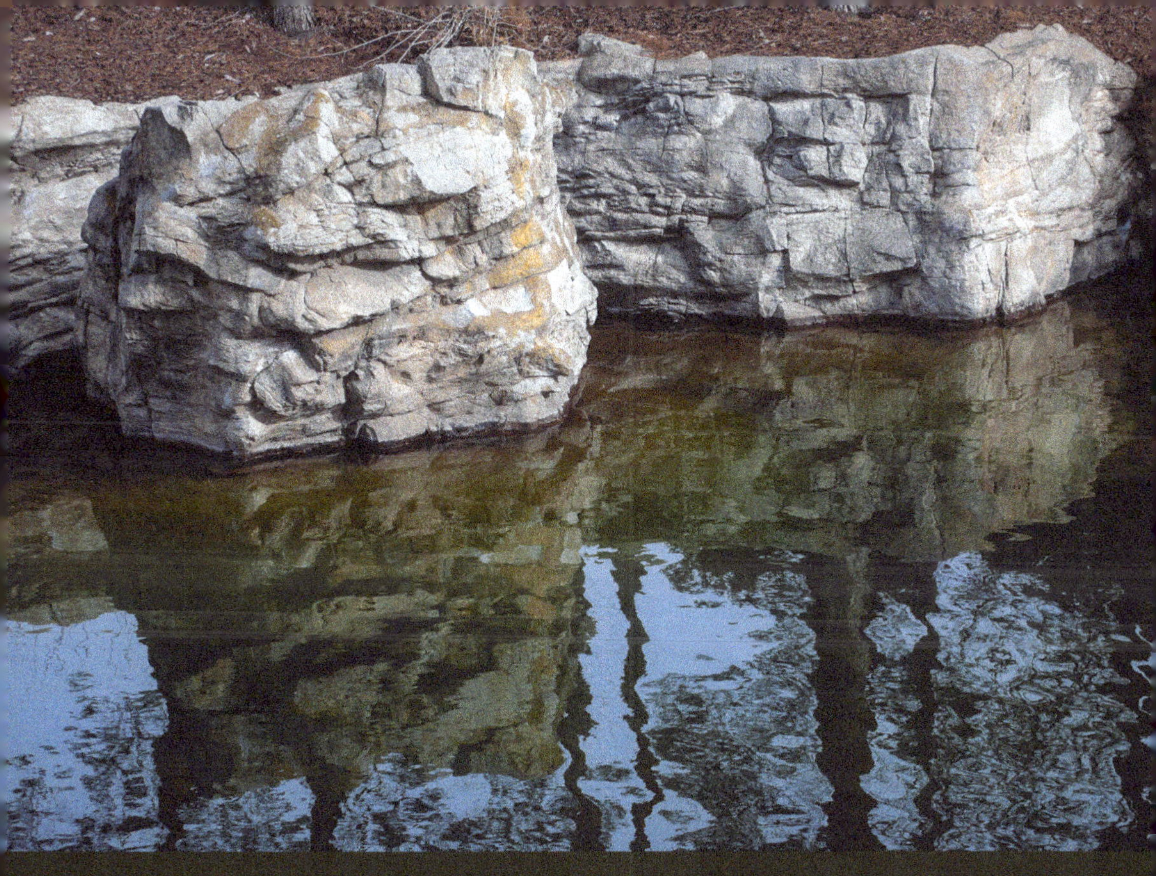

"Darn!" laughed the stones. They had been making fun of passersby for years. "She finally saw us," they said. "Now she'll tell a story about us and other people will think we're wise instead of ordinary blokes."

Seasons came and went. Leaves swelled. Birds bounced on Bruno's branches. He loved his life but wished the tiny new limb was sprouting somewhere besides between his eyes.

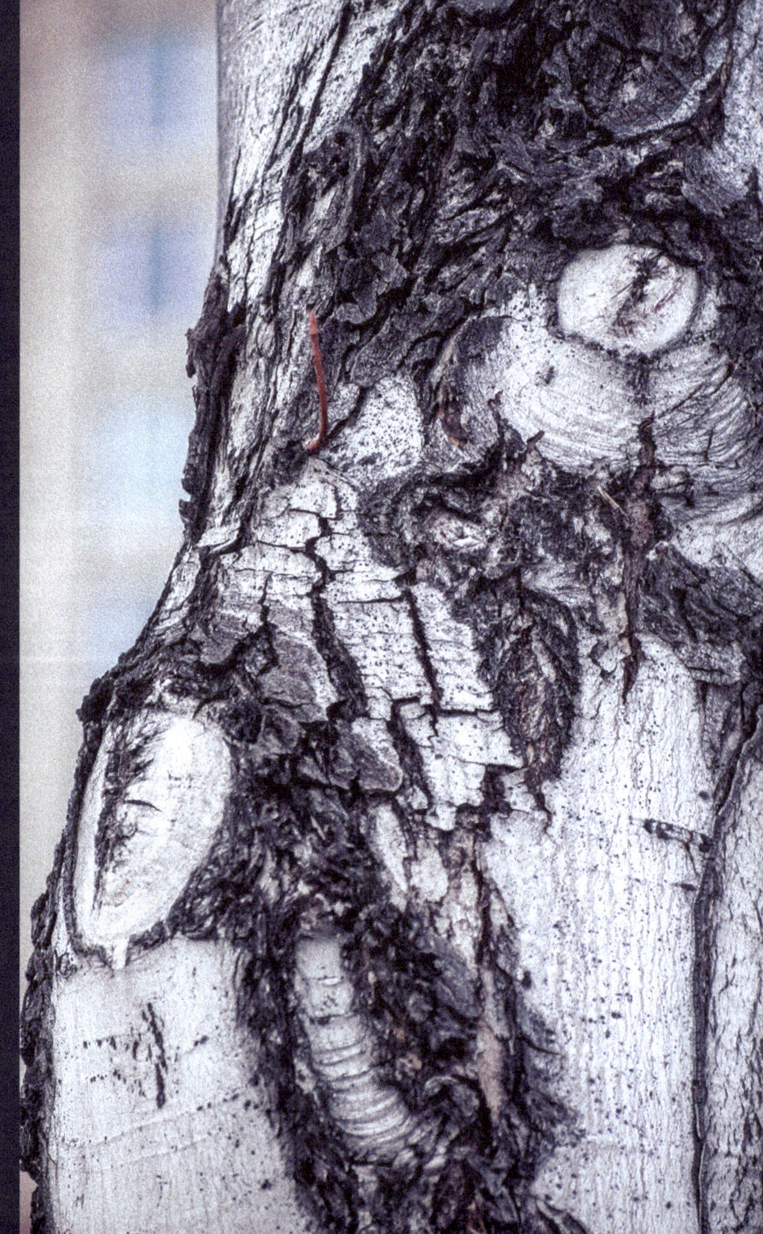

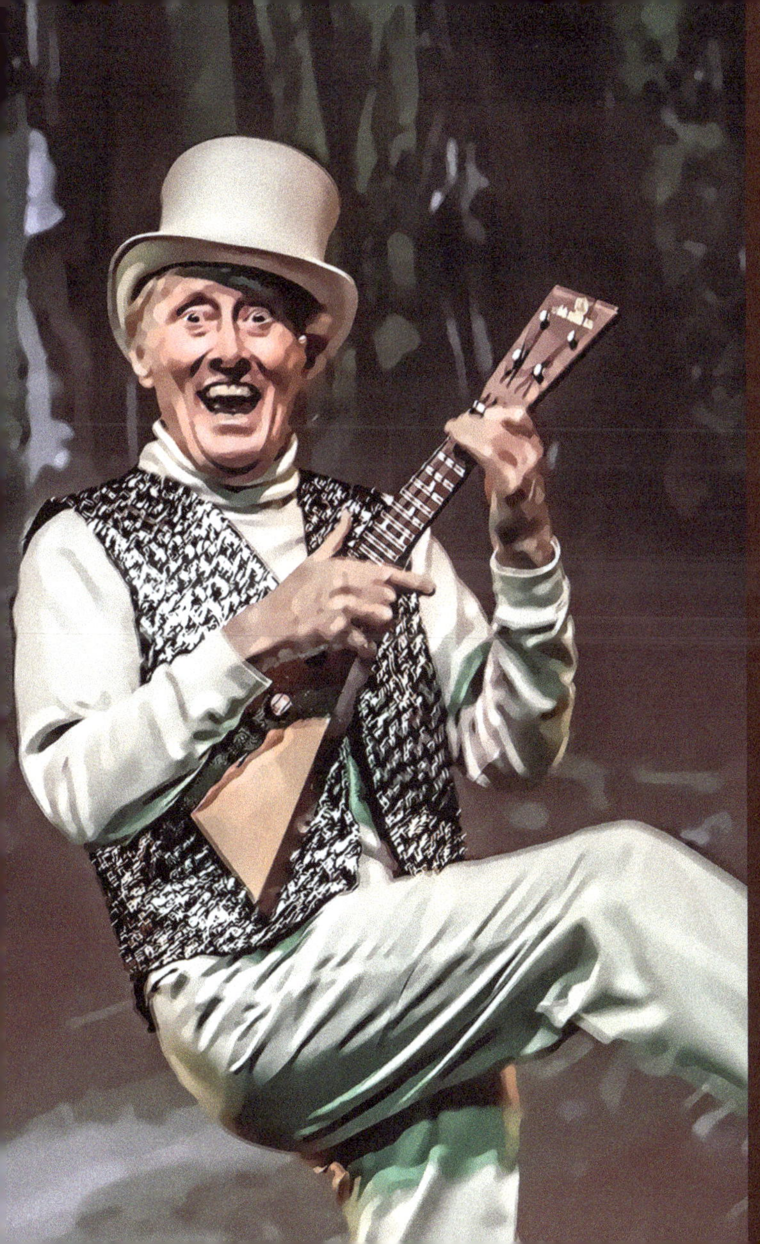

Robin's friends were inspired by his joy. "I'm three quarters* of the way," he said. "Parts of me are still amazing." It gave them a new way to think about their own aging.

*3/4 of a century old

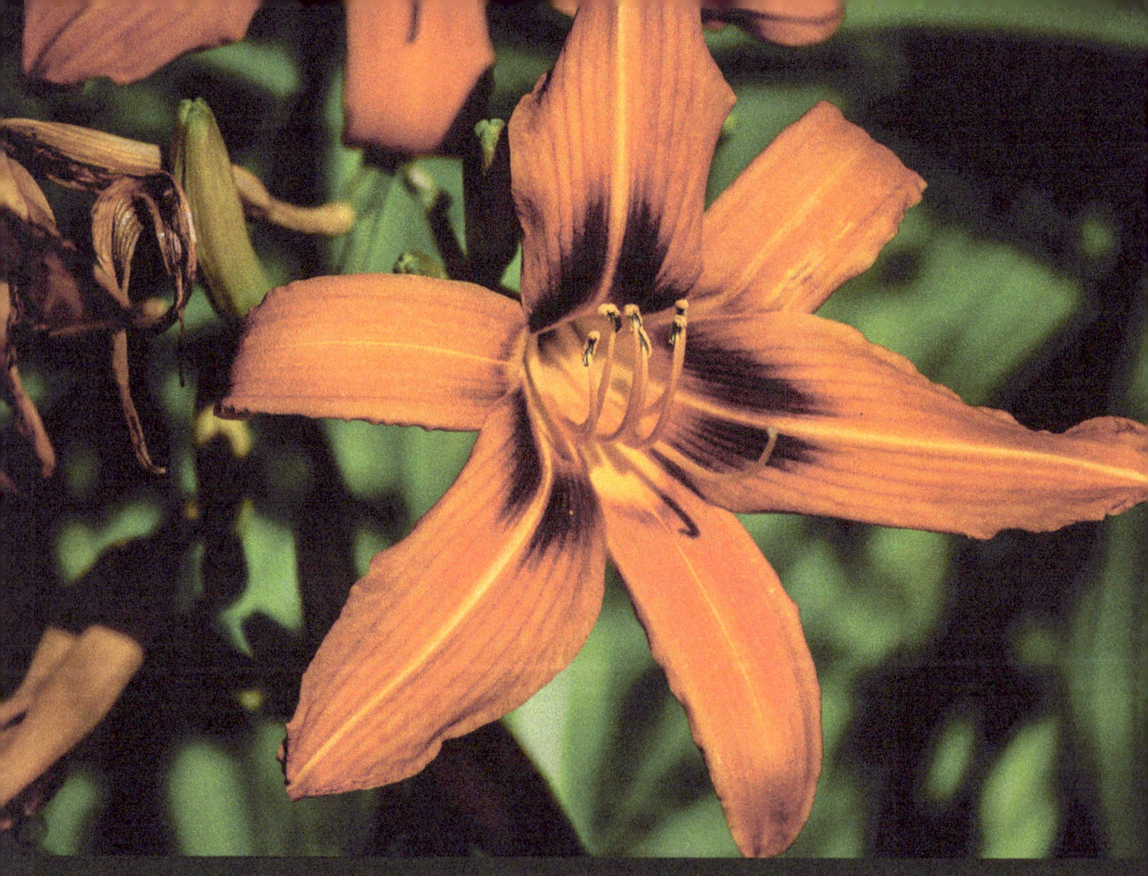

Lily's petals were different sizes and lengths. When she danced with Wind, she moved in ways only possible for a flower so singular. She was the envy of the lilies.

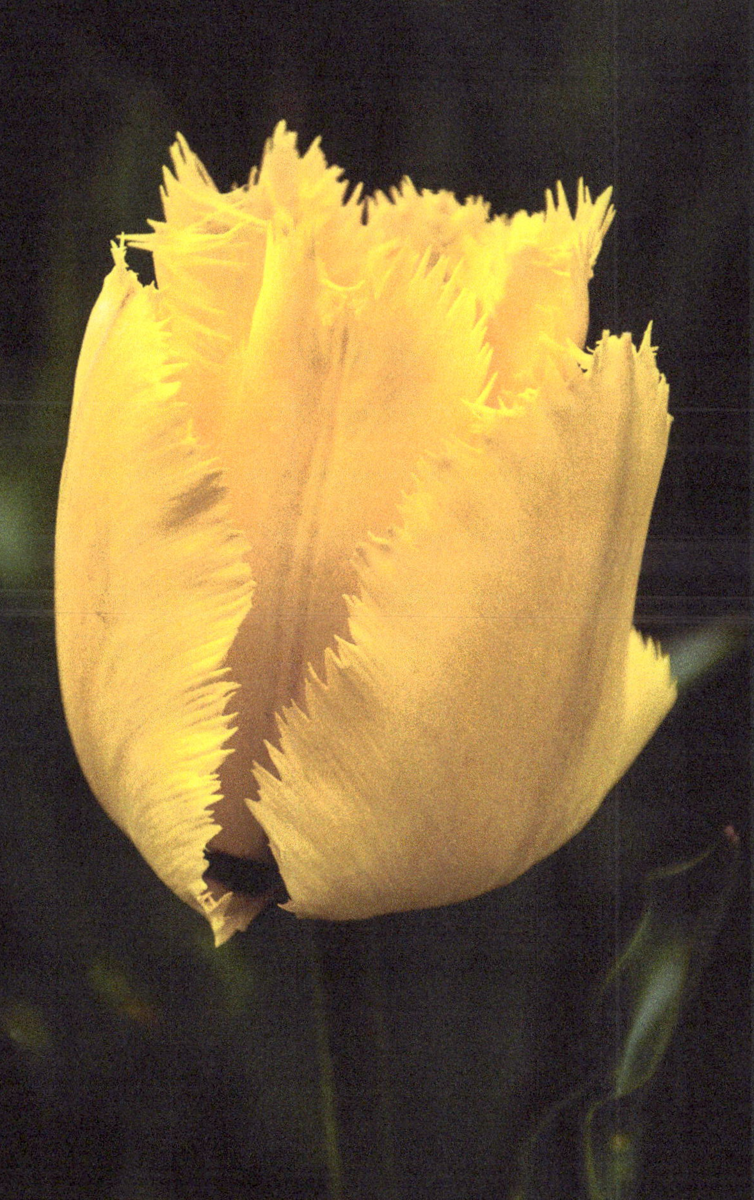

The tulips around her gasped. "Your feathery petals are stunning," they exclaimed. She smiled shyly, grateful for their loving attention.

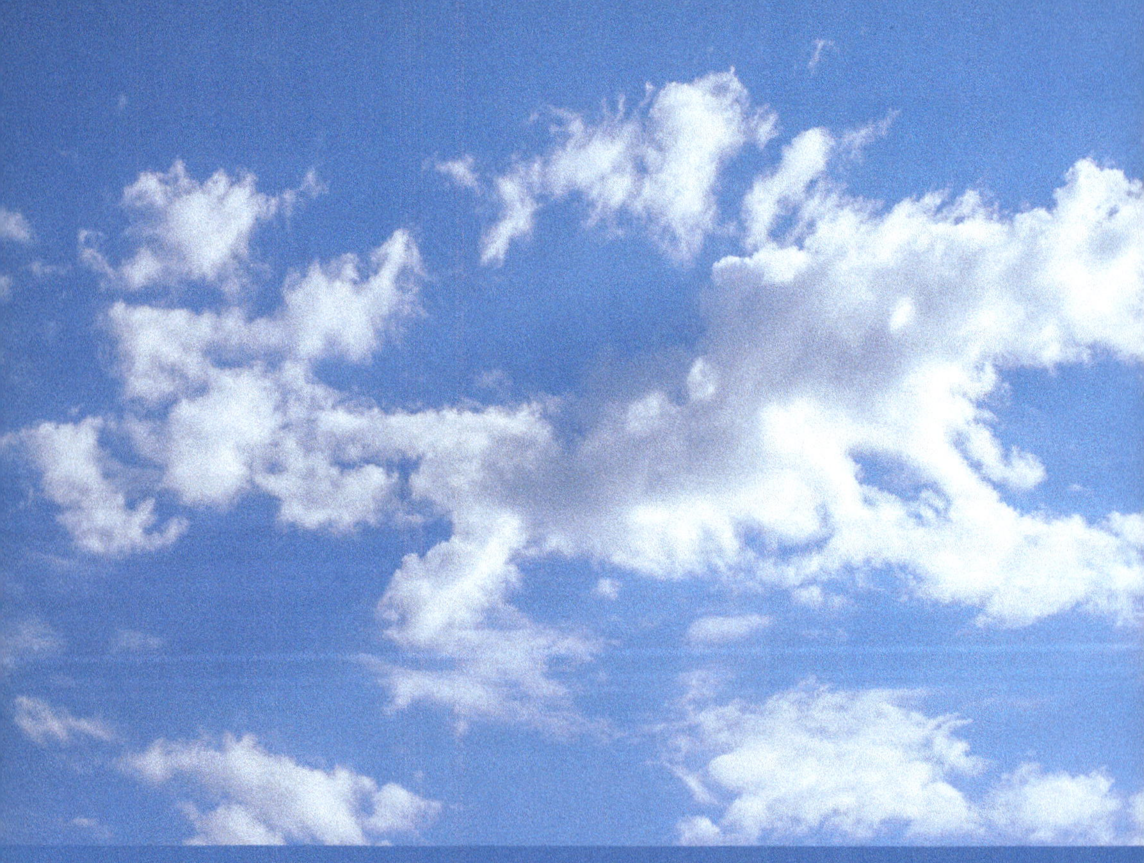

Waldo was playing Dog. He was so pleased with himself, he laughed. That stretched his jaw, shortened his legs, and ruined the effect. He didn't care. Shapes were his favorite game. He would re-form into something else.

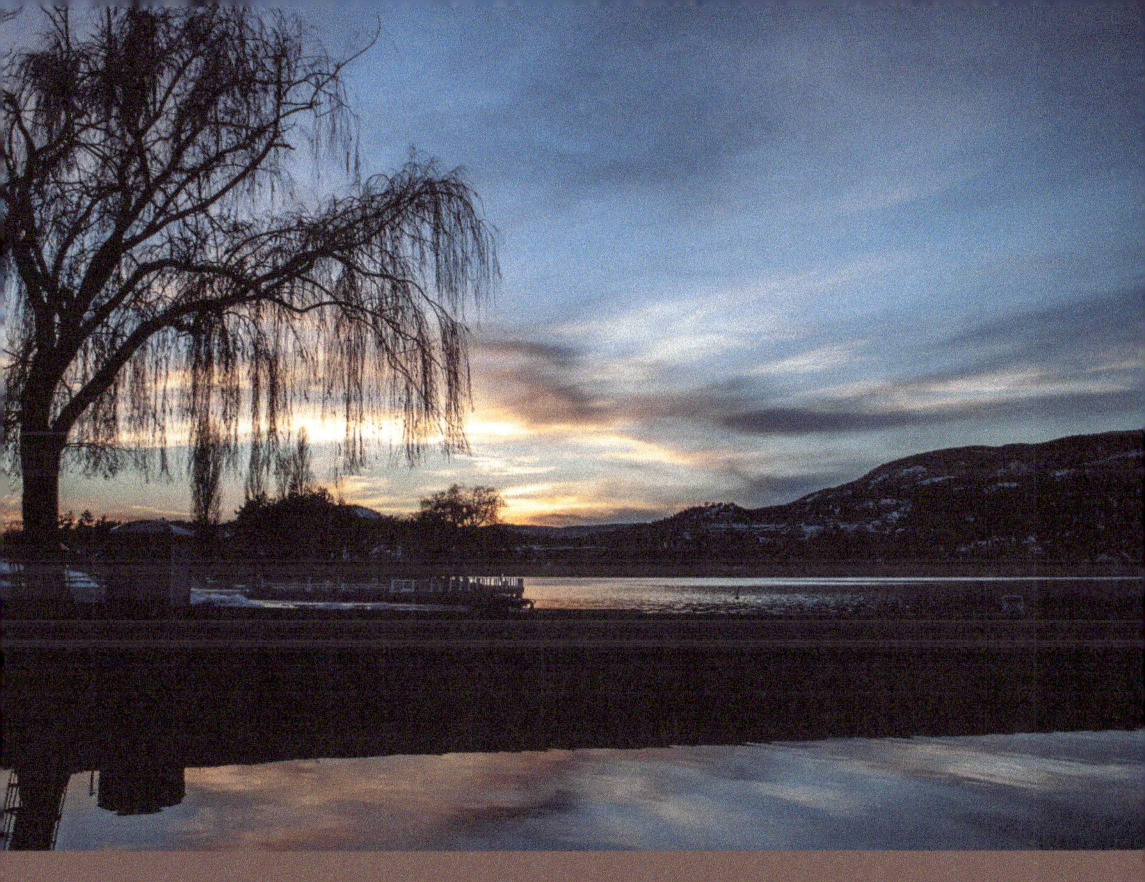

After the city people gave Dog Willow a bad haircut, she craved the darkest nights. Then she overheard passersby admire the tracery of her slender limbs against the setting sun. She lost her fear of aging and waved her graceful arms against the deep orange and blue of the sky.

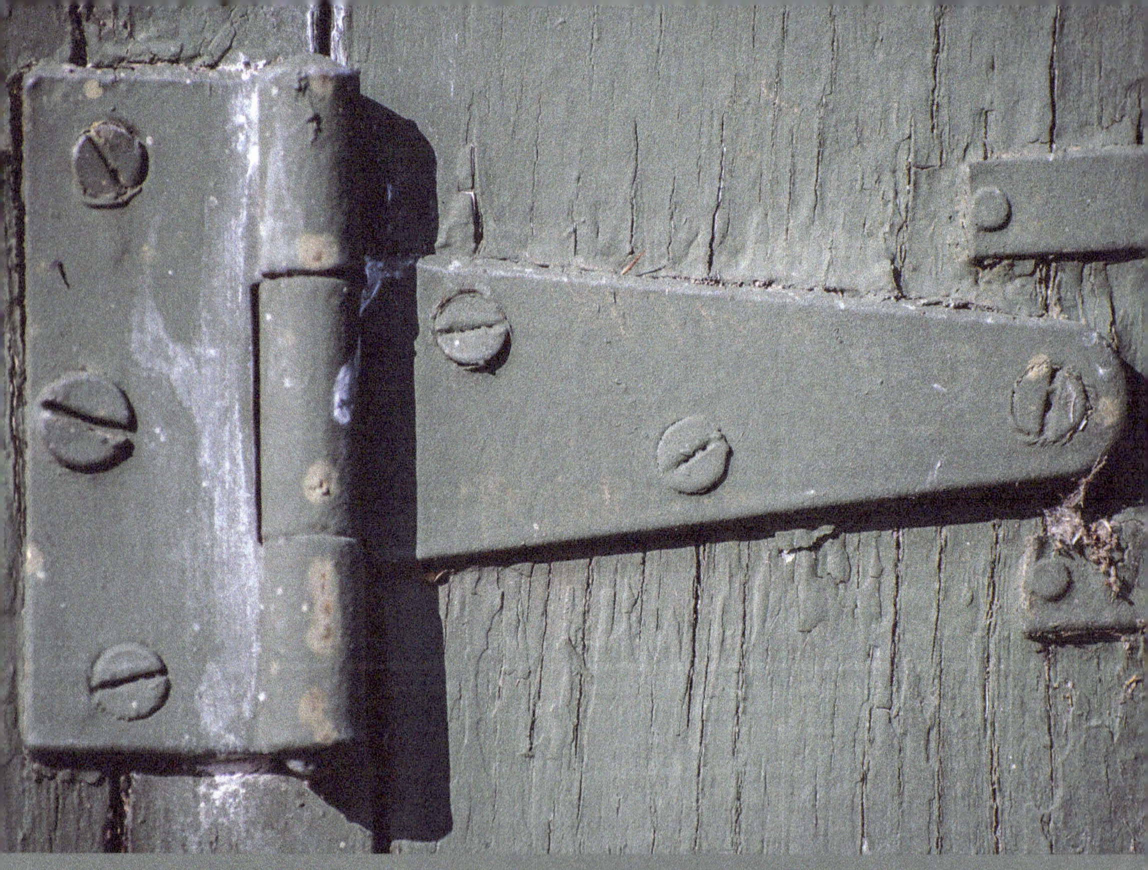

Beneath its many coats of paint, the wood of the garage door was rotting away. Hinge held tightly to it, not wanting to lose her old friend.

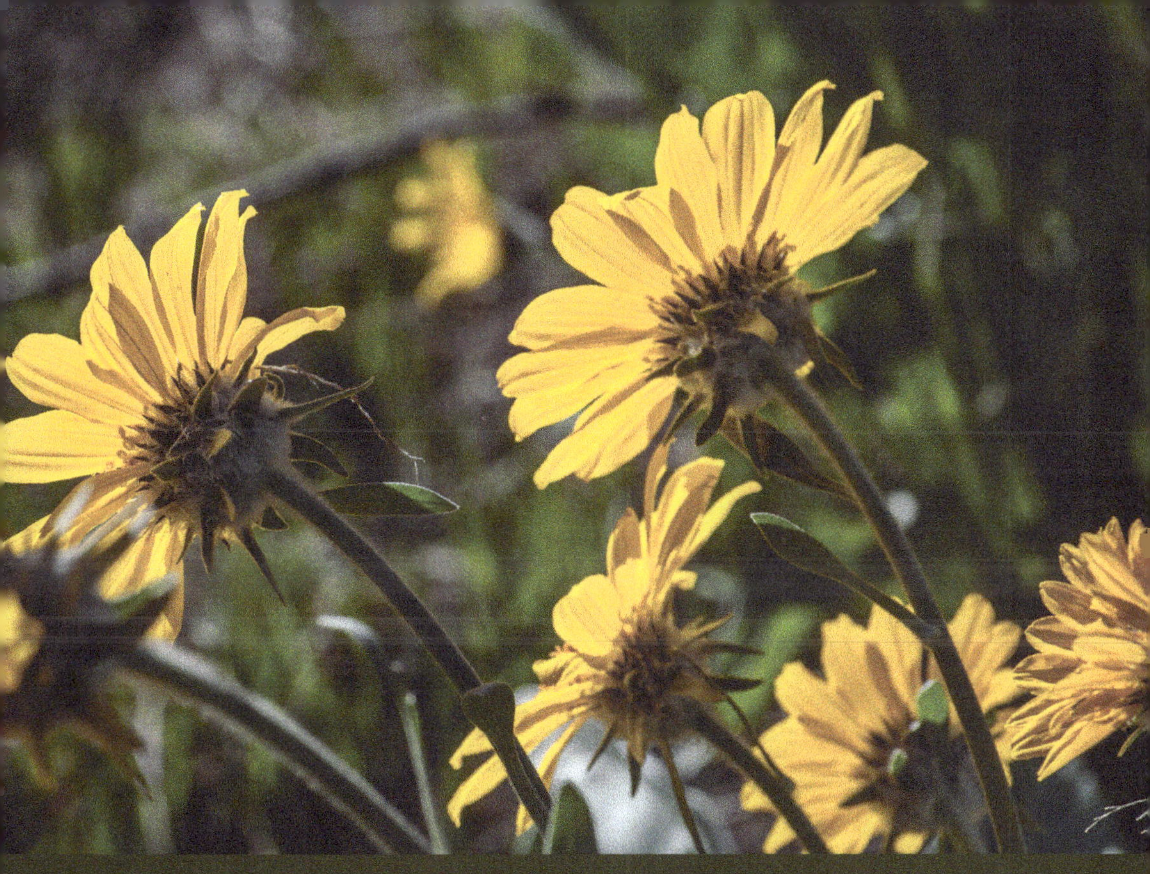

They unfolded their petals to the sun and basked in the admiration of the humans who flocked to see them. "Our life is short," they mused, "but, oh, the pleasure we give in that time."

When their sisters began fading away, the remaining siblings decided to celebrate life rather than regret its passing. Using the dying blossoms as arms, they invited sun and bees to play.

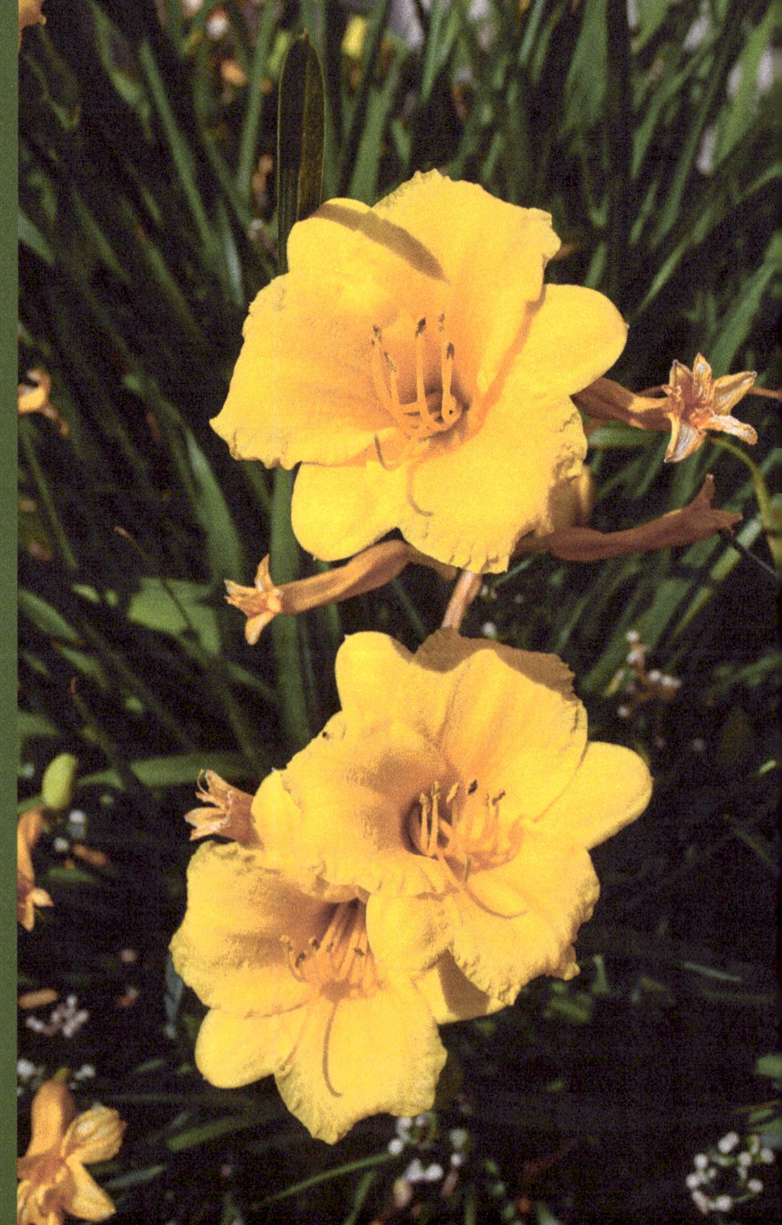

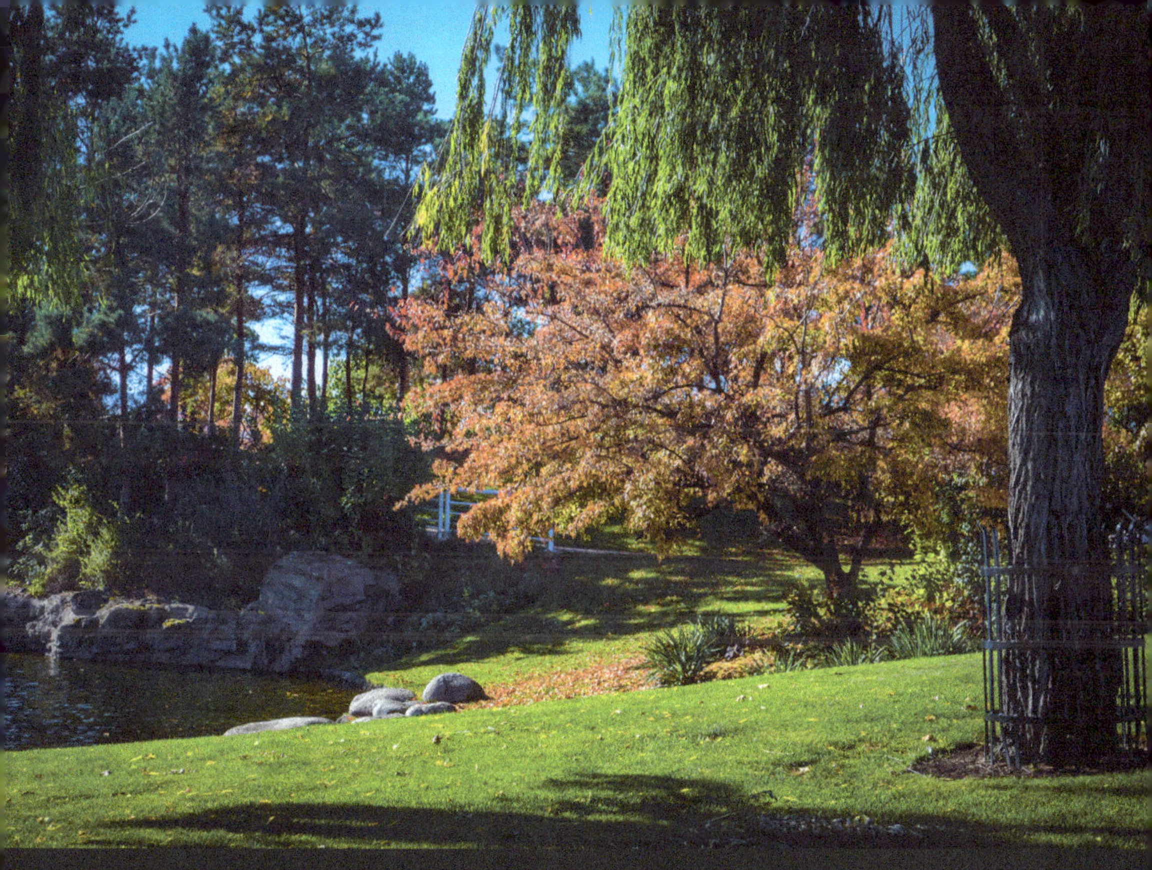

All summer the tree was a quiet green. When he felt the first autumnal chill, he stepped into his full glory. He became a glowing promise, a reminder that every season was fleeting.

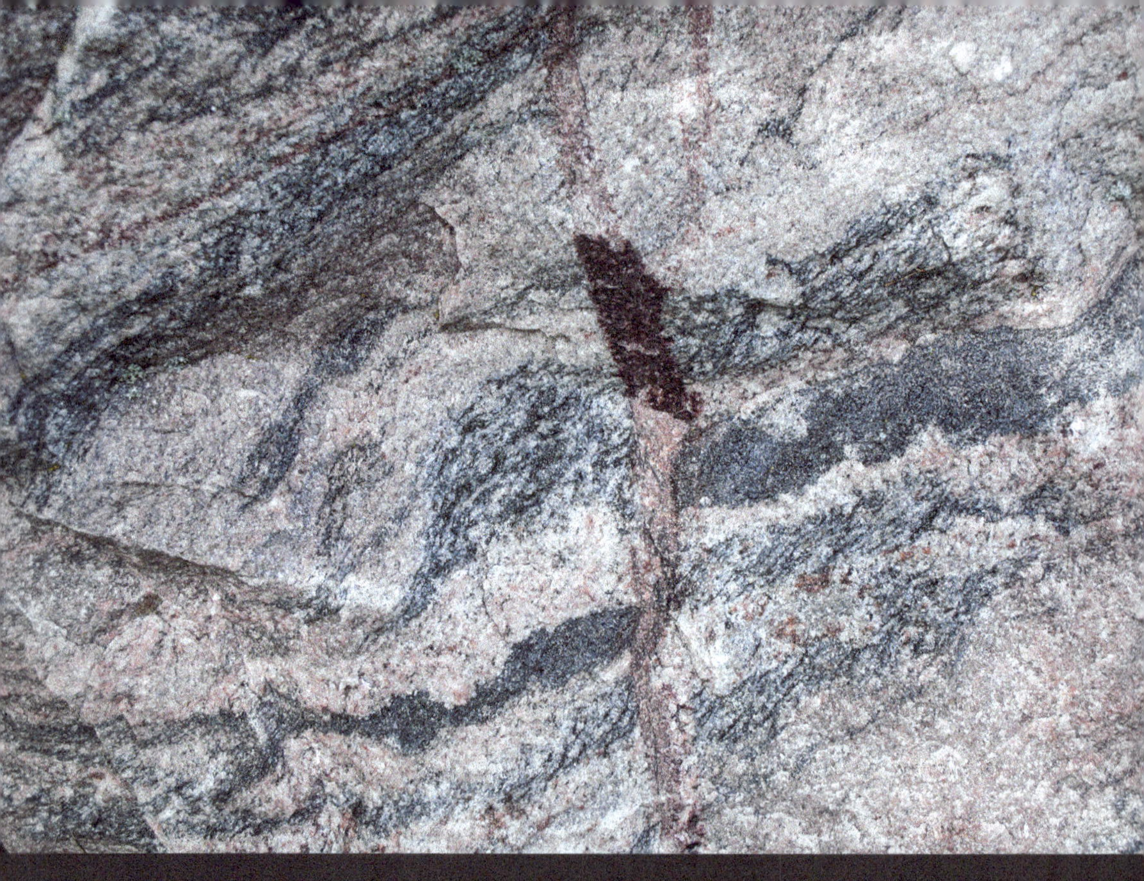

Rock Tree had been in this place for a long time.
But things had changed once earth scrapers tore
him away from his underground home. He did
not like all the changes, but he did like the light.

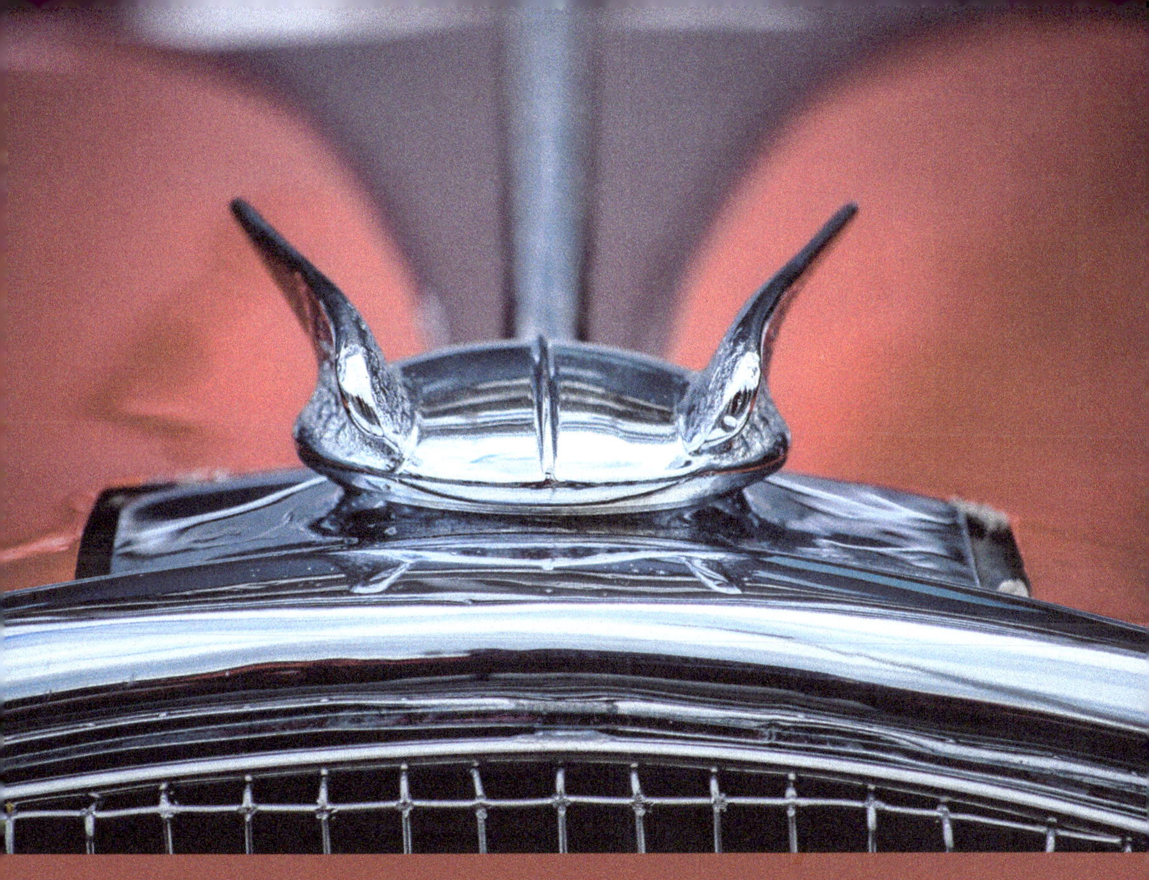

He was a shape shifter, not an ordinary hood ornament. Some days he was a superhero helmet. Today he and Light were creating a winged frog head.

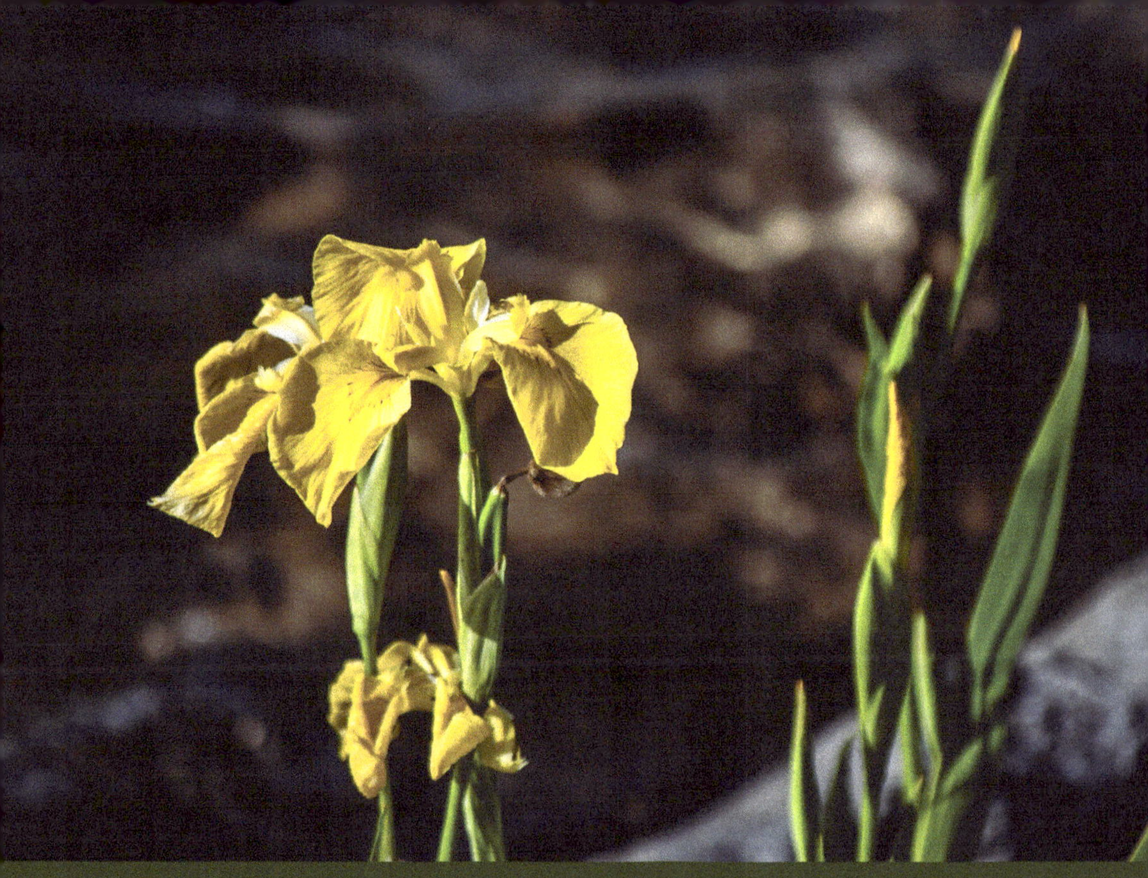

The iris could feel it. Their days of glorious blooming were coming to a close. But within them they sensed the stirrings of the next generation, not pushing them aside but joining them in the long parade of Life As It Unfolds.

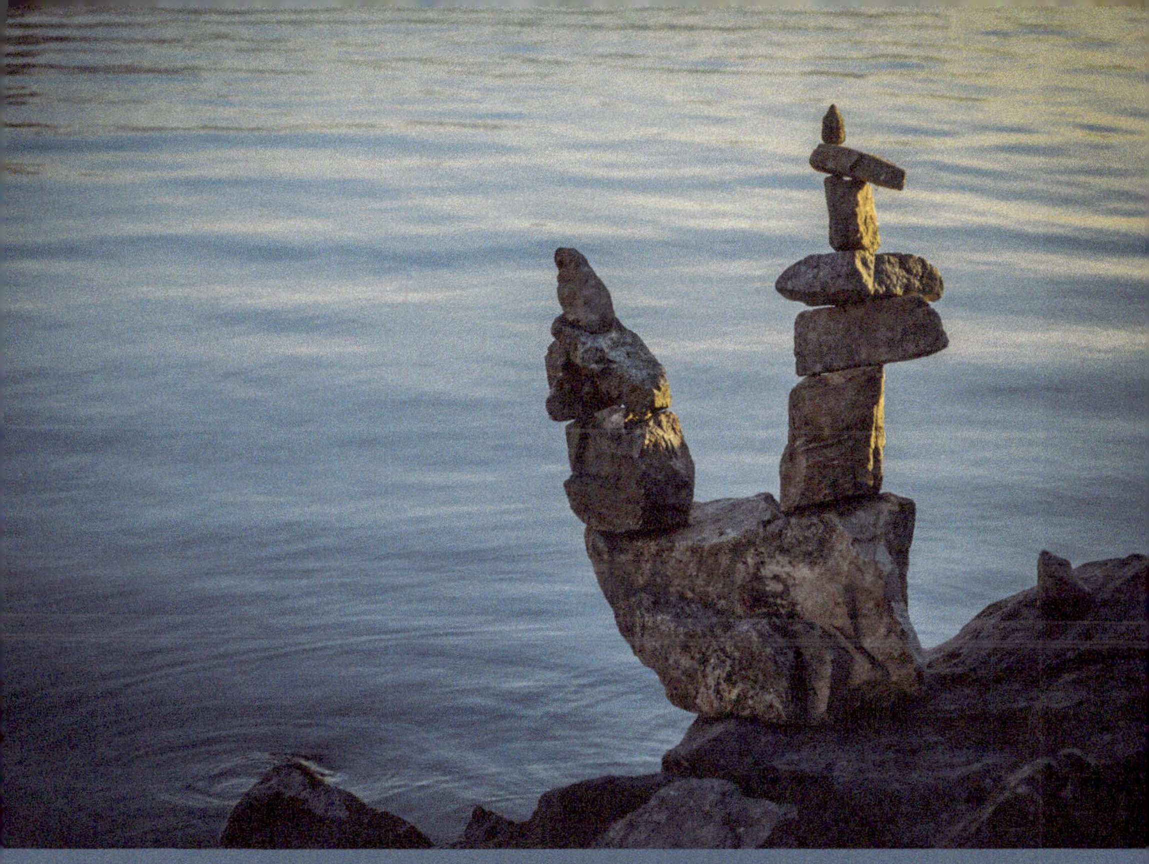

Sun warmed the inukshuk stones and made them smile. They had not had so much fun since they were carved out of their home mountains.

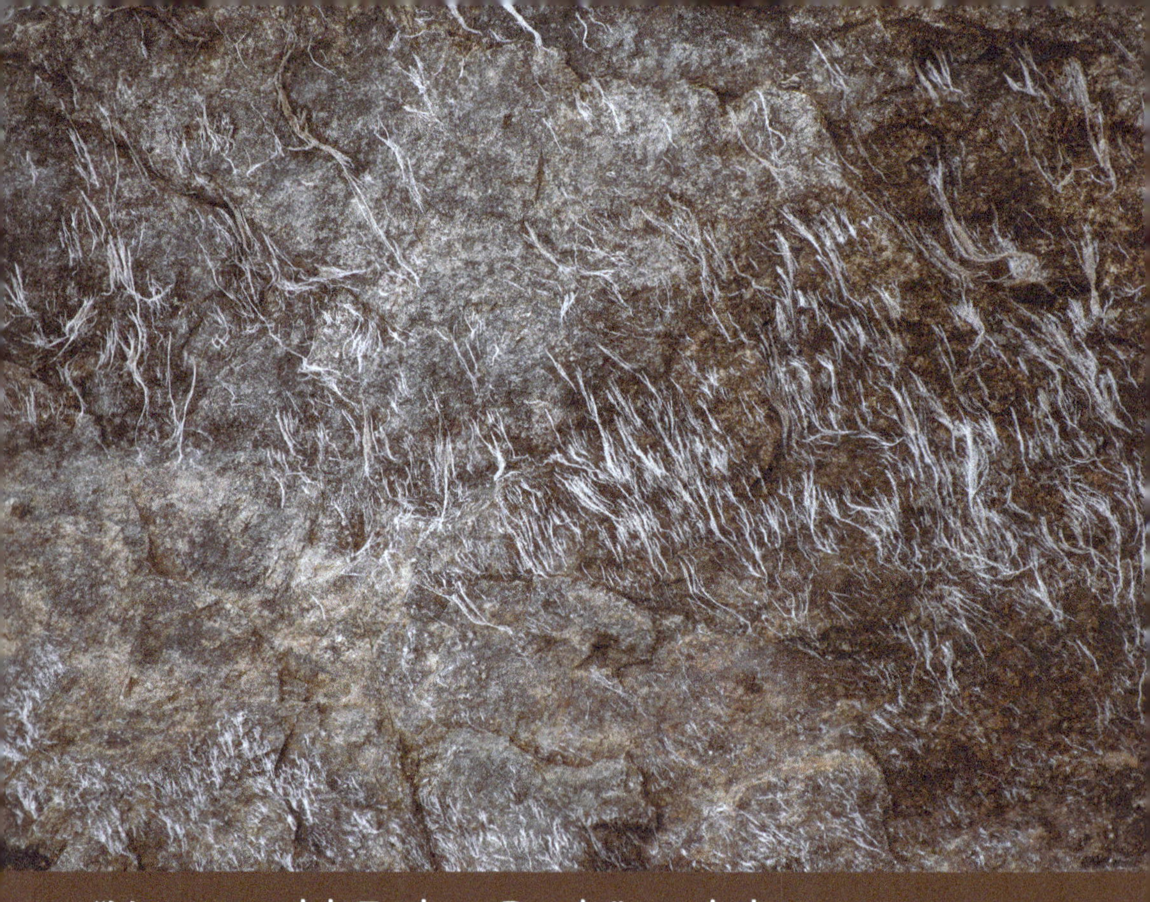

"You are old, Father Rock," said the mossy tendrils. Rock smiled indulgently, knowing he would be there long after anything that clung to him had passed on.

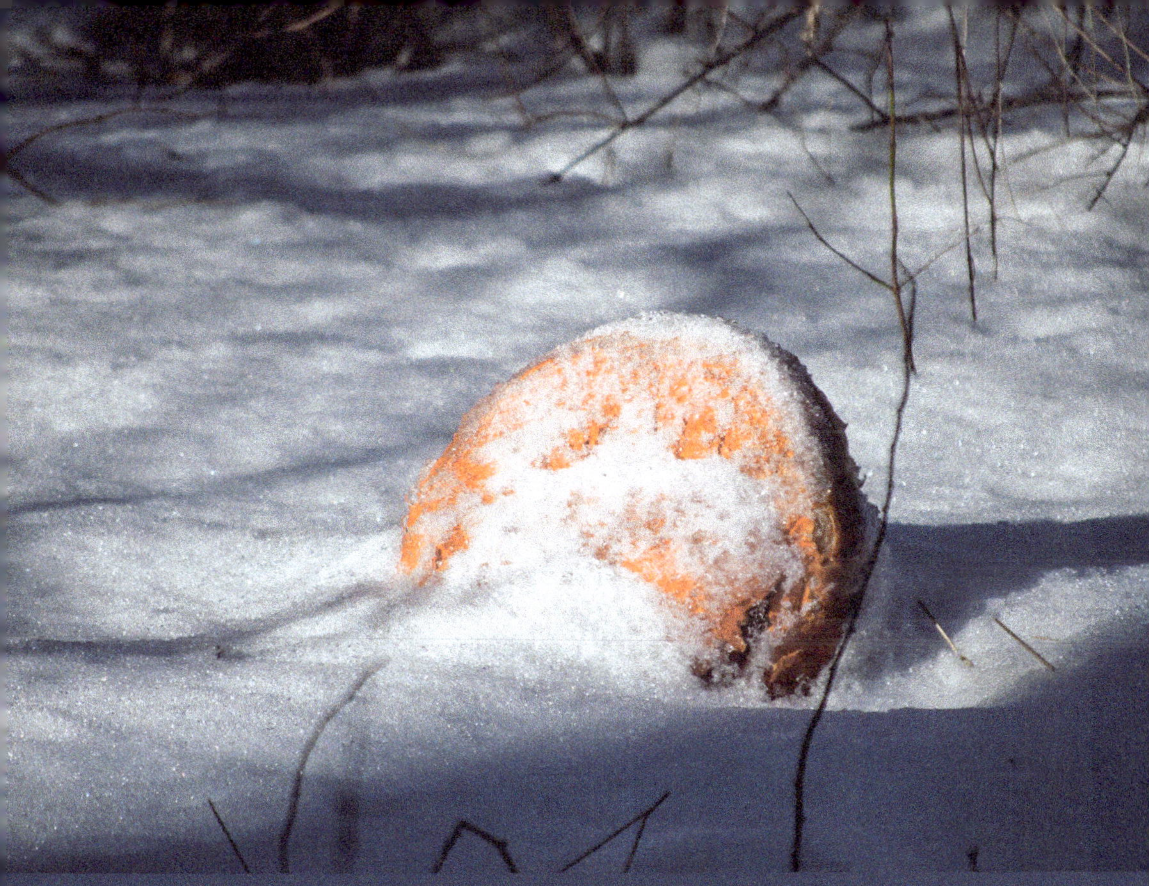

Pumpkin dreamed through the long winter. As the snow began to melt, she prepared for her final act, when she would provide food for migrating birds.

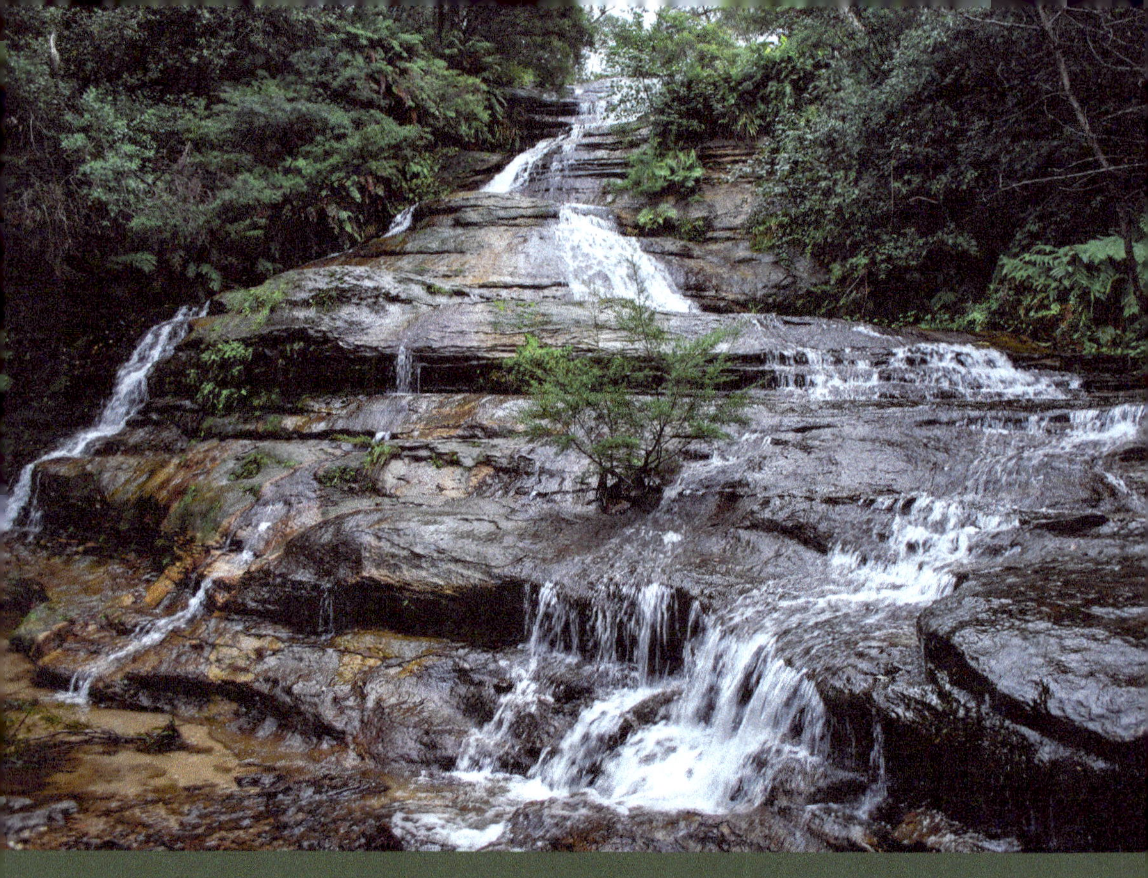

Centuries passed, and still Water showed her love for Rock by gently tracing every line, ledge and crack of her beloved.

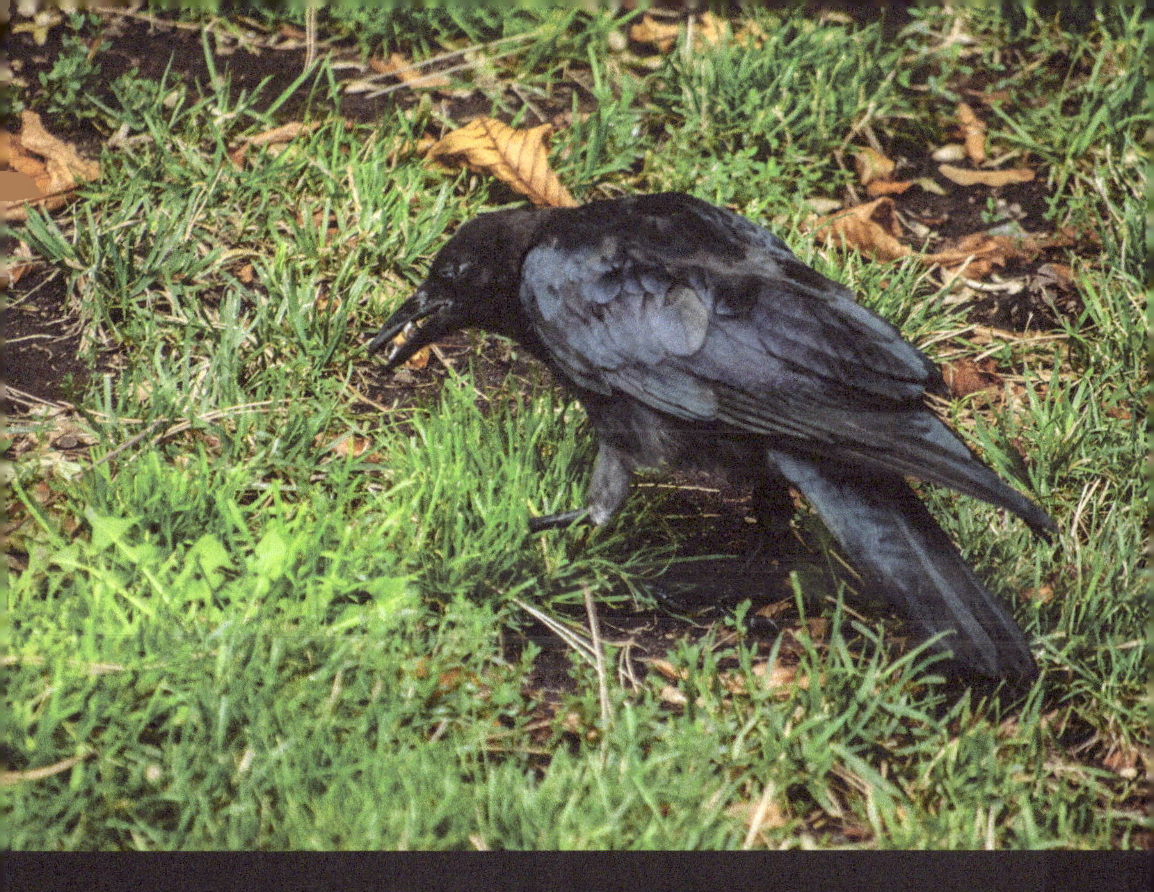

Crow hopped through the grass, searching for dinner. Her eyes were rheumy, but the rest of her senses were as sharp as ever. She knew the younger crows secretly admired her hop dance and the sheen of her feathers.

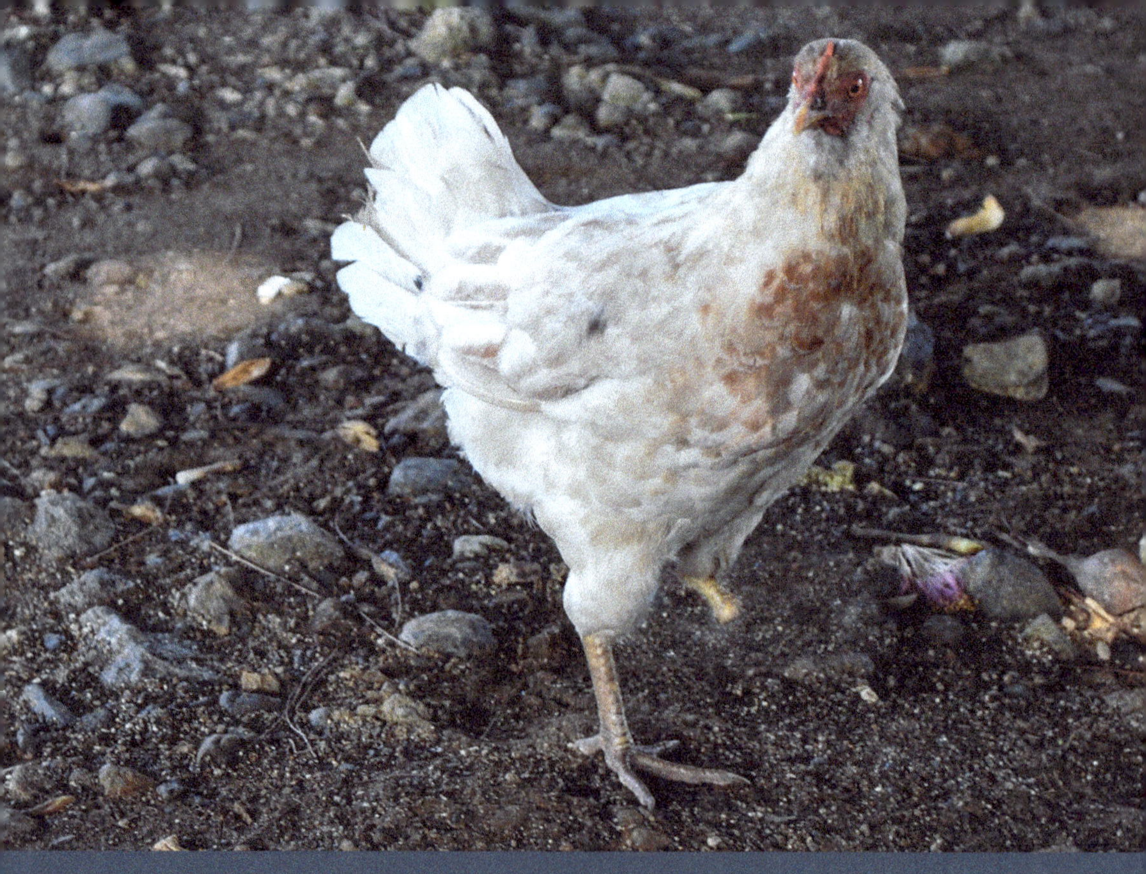

Bijou moved with such ease few of the people
who saw her searching for food realized she had
only one leg.

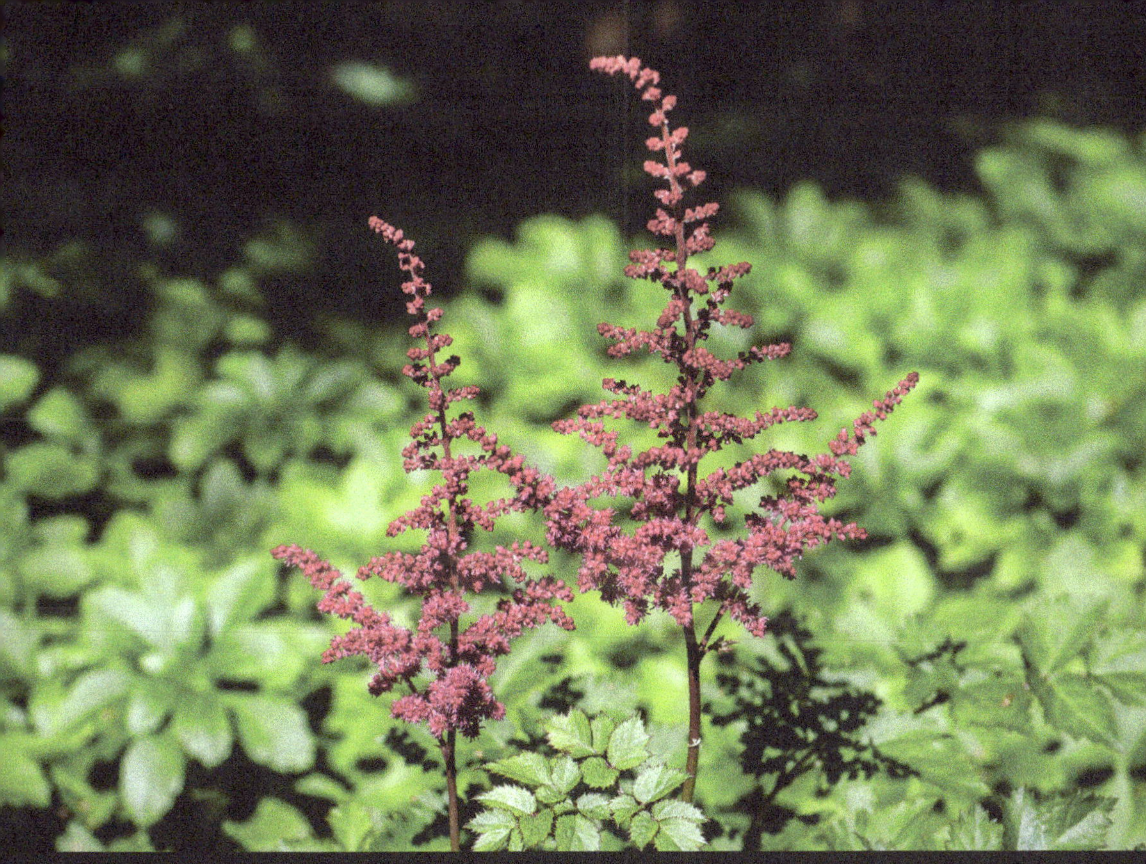

When they emerged from the green surrounding them, they were stunned by their own, bright beauty. They looked at each other in wonder, signaled to the wind, and began to dance.

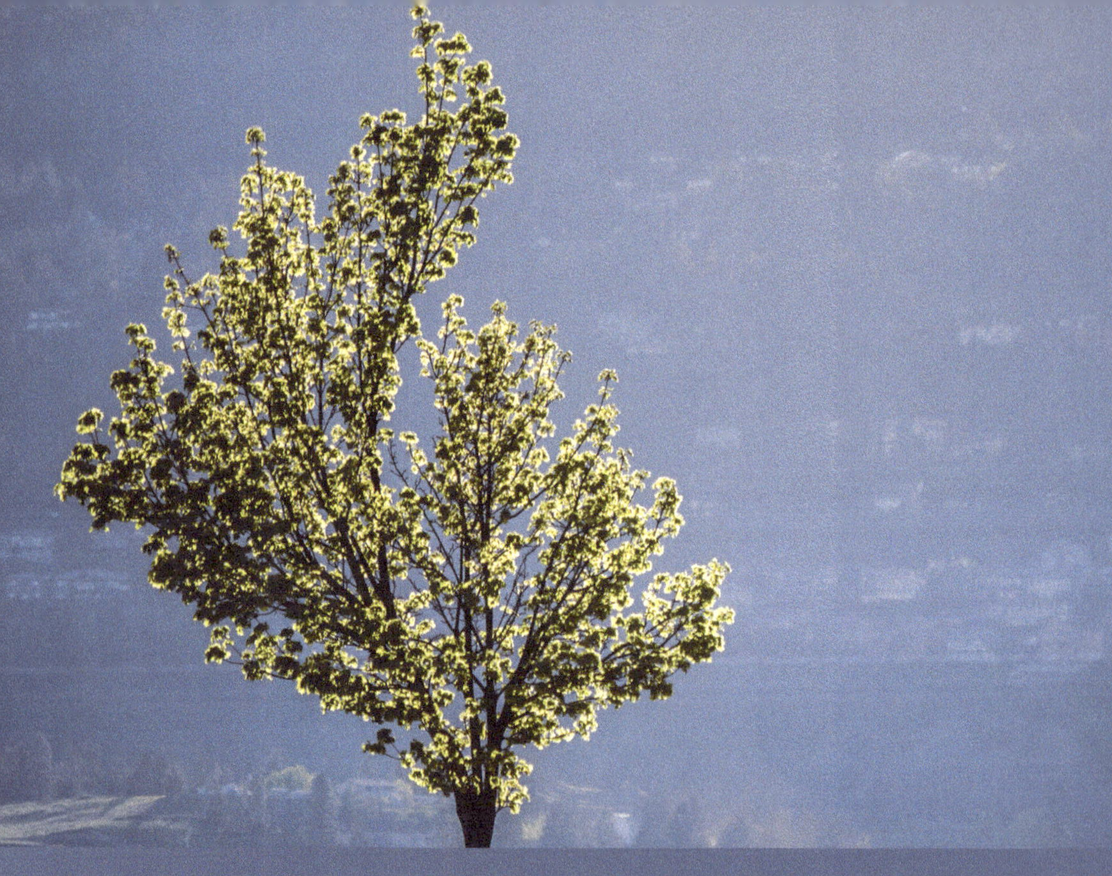

Sometimes the nearby trees mocked her irregular shape. But when the sun shone through her spring leaves, their teasing voices fell silent. As they looked at her in awe, she remembered her own beauty.

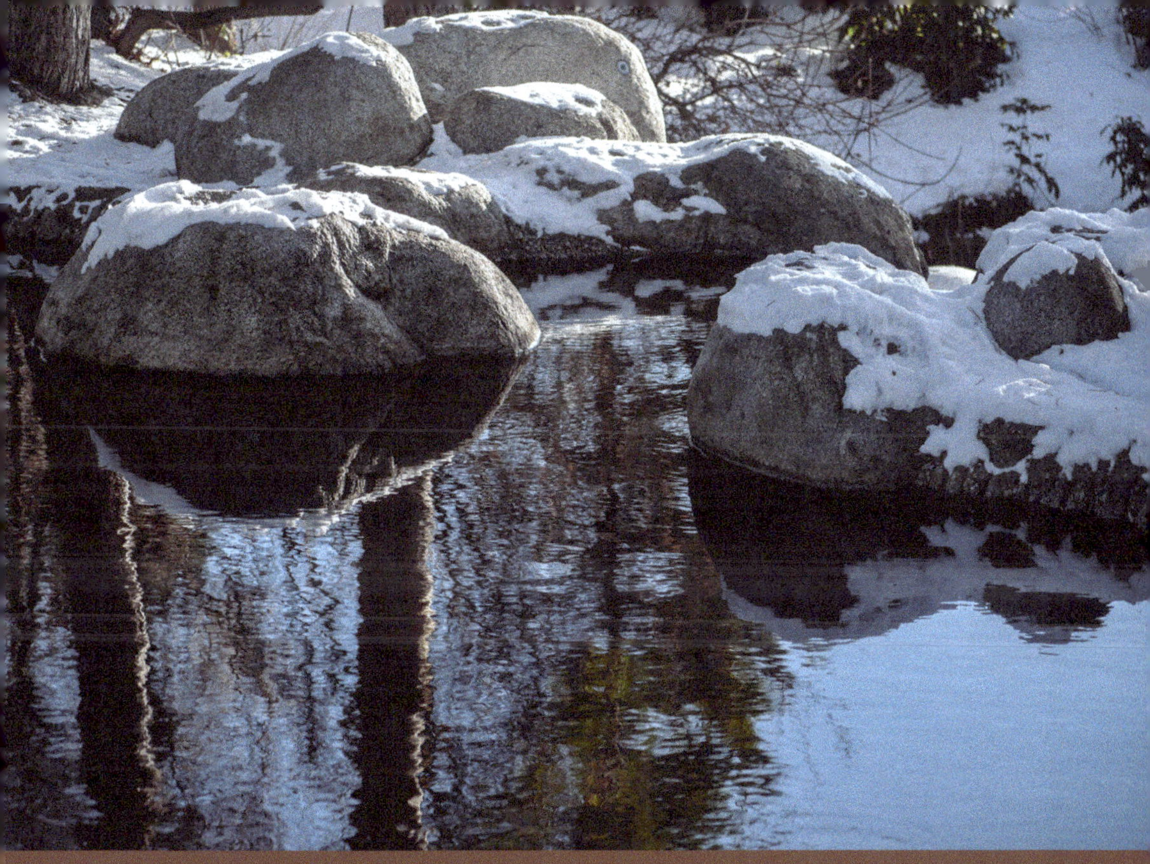

Stone gazed at her round belly, her slender legs. She knew the "legs" were reflections of the trees behind her, but for a moment she was a crane-like figure, capable of walking, leaping, and adventuring.

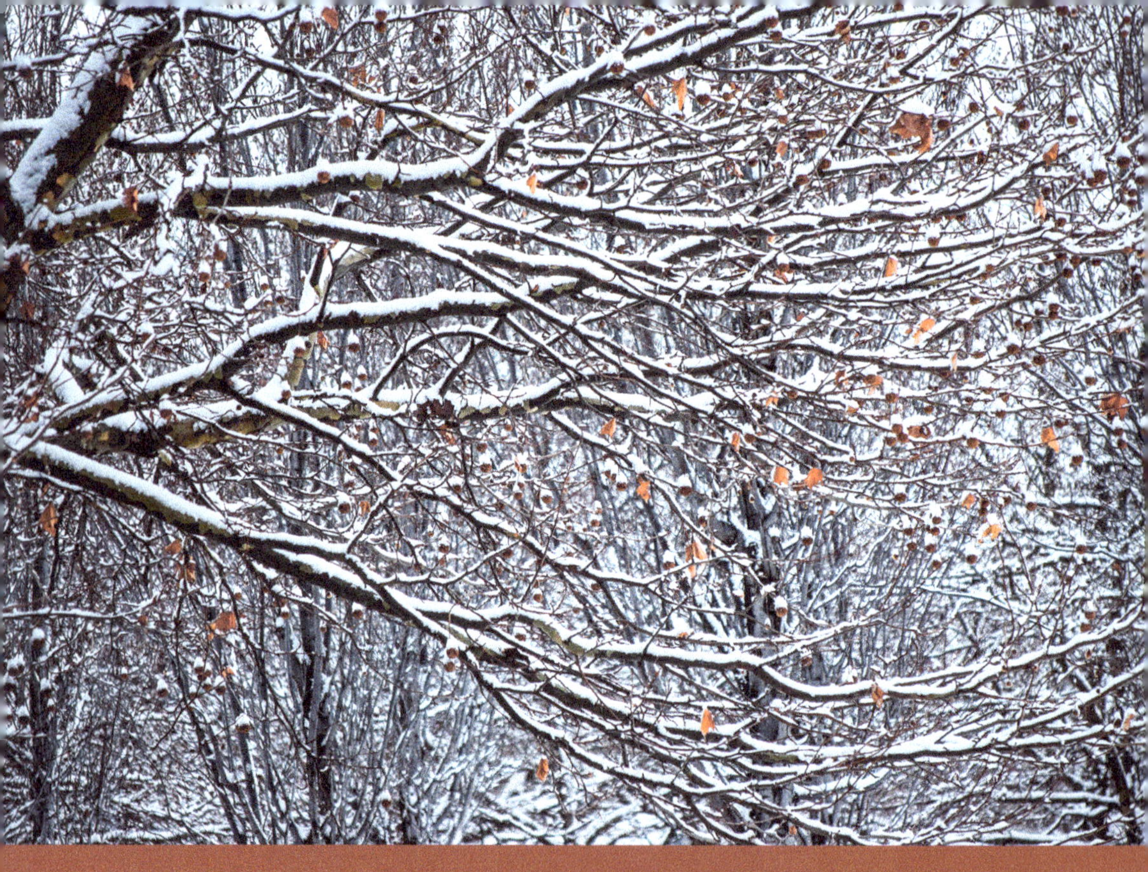

Plane Tree remained perfectly still. She could hear Wind in the distance. Until he came she would hold Snow in her embrace, while the year's last leaves looked on in delight.

ABOUT THE AUTHOR

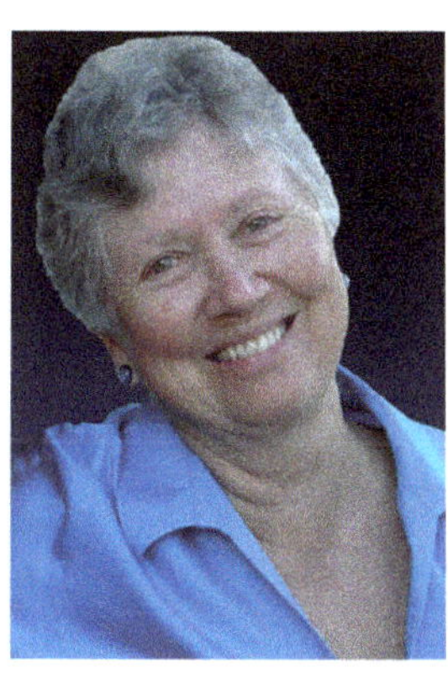

Cathryn Wellner is a writer, photographer and storyteller living in Kelowna, British Columbia, Canada.

Recent books by Cathryn include:
That Tree Talked to Me
Hope Wins
Feisty Aging
In the Hug of Hills
Millie's Feathered Foster Family
Turkey Baby and the Hungry Hawk
Turkey Baby Finds Her Magic
Cloud Talk

You can find links to these and her other books at cathrynwellner.com. Contact her at cathryn@cathrynwellner.com or 778-478-2760. Her photographs can be found on her Web site, as well as on Facebook and Instagram.

BE A BOOK REVIEW ANGEL

If you enjoyed this book, please post a review on Amazon or Goodreads. Share it with friends and rave about it on social media. You can contact the author at cathryn@cathrynwellner.com.

Authors rely on their readers to help spread the word about books they like. People who review books are special kinds of reader angels. I guarantee when you review this book, or any other book that has given you pleasure in any way, you'll feel those wings poking out your back. Look closely in the mirror, and you might even see a halo.

Credits

Cover fonts: Saltash and BasicSans. Interior font: Bw Surco. Logo font: Ed's Market. Cover background by Pixie Paints Fine Art Textures. Tropical image on dedication page by StarJam. (All licensed through DesignCuts.)

The book was designed in Photoshop.

Thank you to the amazingly creative people who designed all of the above.

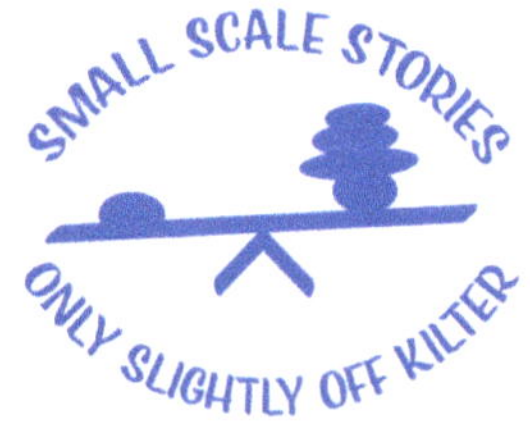